Awesome Internet Sites for Kids

By Sandra Antoniani, Robyn Rektor,
Lisa Slage Robinson, Fiona Rowan

With contributions by Deanna Phillips and Laurie Smith
Book design and illustrations by Terri Lee

Awesome Internet Sites for Kids
A Publication of Ride the Wave Media, Inc.
14 Cross Street
Dundas, ON
Canada L9H 2R4

Contact us at: 1-866-628-9539
www.smork.com

ISBN 0-9731020-0-4

Printed at WebCom Limited in Toronto, on 100% recycled paper (containing 100% post consumer content).

CONTENTS

SMORK's Mission Statement

To help kids and their parents have a safe, fun and educational Internet experience while encouraging children to become environmentally aware and responsible global citizens.

Smork Safe URLs

Some of Smork's Awesome Sites have VERY long website addresses. We want to make it easy for you to get to the site you want, so we have given each site a short and easy Smork Address. Just type the Smork Address, and we'll take you directly to that site. If you make a mistake, we'll take you to Smork's OOPS!!! Page, where you can choose your site from our drop down menu. Don't want to type at all? Visit www.smork.com to click and surf!

Smork's Age Ranking System (-/+)

Smork's Awesome Sites have been chosen for kids ages 5–13. Since some sites are more likely to be enjoyed by younger kids, some older, and some are terrific for just about anyone, we have marked our sites to let you know where each site ranks. The (-) symbol is for sites that will likely appeal to the younger kids in our group. A site marked with the (+) symbol will most likely appeal to the older kids. Sites marked with (-/+) symbol means that all kids will enjoy the site.

Do You Know Where Your Children Surf?

Smork's research team has made every effort to find sites that will provide your children with an interesting, inspiring and safe Internet experience. There is, however, no substitute for parental supervision and participation in a child's Internet adventure. Parents need to take the time to discuss Internet use with their children and to ensure that their kids develop safe surfing practices. Smork is just a map—Parents are the real Guides. (KIDS, if you're reading this—talk to your parents about your Internet use and don't give out information about yourself on any websites, unless your parents have reviewed the site with you.)

More Legal Stuff—Content, E-commerce and More...Caveat Emptor!

While every effort has been made to ensure accuracy, the information contained in the sites listed in this book is subject to change without notice. In other words, we can only tell you what was there when we looked. Given the ever changing nature of the Internet, it is possible that the contents or existence of websites will change during the lifetime of this publication. All site descriptions are provided for informational purposes only (we liked the site; you can decide when you get there, if you agree). Smork's site selections were based on presentation and information offered at the time of our visit. We do not conduct consumer transactions at any listed site (this is the **Caveat Emptor** part). Individual sites are completely responsible for their own content and security. SMORK strongly encourages readers to exercise care in their interactions or consumer transactions with any of the sites listed. Neither SMORK nor any officer or employee can be held responsible for individual interpretations, representations or actual experiences with individual merchants on the information contained in this guide.

WHEW! Enjoy your surfing.

Animal Tracks

Can you guess what animals made these three tracks?

Check out **www.bear-tracker.com** for more animal tracks!

Courtesy of Kim A. Cabrera at www.bear-tracker.com

Hinterland's Who's Who—Canadian Wildlife Service

This site shows Canadian wildlife in action. Watch one-minute video clips of Canadian birds and mammals and see everything from an Arctic Fox to a Peregrine Falcon. Read or print Fact Sheets that tell each animal's story. Learn about appearance, habitats, feeding and predators. Great for school projects! (-/+)

www.AN1.smork.com
www.cws-scf.ec.gc.ca/hww-fap/eng_ind.html

How to Love Your Dog

This site is dedicated to the best friend you may ever have, your dog. How to Love Your Dog will prepare you for owning a dog and gives you practical tips about dog behavior and safety. Be responsible for your pet and they'll love you right back. (-/+)

www.AN2.smork.com   www.geocities.com/~kidsanddogs

Kratt's Creatures

The Kratt Brothers, Chris and Martin, have their own TV show—and this is their website. Look at Creatures from the five continents in the Creature World section. Can you guess if a Chewybaccus Biggus is a real creature or not? Play Creature or Not and find out. (-)

www.AN3.smork.com   www.pbs.org/kratts/world

The Life of Birds

Learn about the extraordinary life of birds. Find out what 9000 bird species have in common, how they evolved, how they parent and why they sing. You'll never call anyone bird brain again! (+)

www.AN4.smork.com   www.pbs.org/lifeofbirds

Funky Animal Facts

"Sharks don't chew their food; they rip off chunks of meat and swallow them whole. After eating a seal or a sea lion, the great white shark can last a month or two without another big meal."

"Giraffes are the tallest animals in the world. They run 35 miles an hour (56 kilometers an hour)."

"Rather than sucking blood, vampire bats make a small cut with their teeth and then lap up the flowing blood with their tongues. These bats are so light and agile that they are sometimes able to drink blood from an animal for more than 30 minutes without waking it up. The blood sucking does not hurt the animal."

Animal facts courtesy of The National Geographic.com, www.nationalgeographic.com
© 2002 National Geographic Society

Oceanlink

From sensational otters to slimy slugs, you'll meet some strange deep sea creatures on this site. Listen to whales, seals and snapping shrimp. Explore fascinating and mysterious plant and life forms. You'll find out how the moon and sun affect the tides and so much more. Great for school projects. (+)

www.AN5.smork.com   www.oceanlink.island.net

Sea World/Busch Gardens Animal Information Database

Sharks and Whales and Dolphins — Oh My! Visit Sea World's Animal Information Database and learn about creatures that live under the sea. Click on Zoological Park Careers to learn how to become an animal trainer and check out other cool jobs where you get to work with animals. (+)

www.AN6.smork.com   www.seaworld.org/infobook.html

The Electronic Zoo

The Electronic Zoo gives you dozens of links to animal sites. From the Froggy Page under Amphibians to Garfield Online under Fictional Animals, you can search for just about every type of fish, bird, reptile or primate here. Listen to Whale Songs under Sounds or browse through pictures, paintings and drawings in the Images section. (+)

www.AN7.smork.com   http://netvet.wustl.edu/ssi.htm

Virtual Wildlife

Does an ostrich really bury its head in the sand? Are snapping turtles police detectives? Choose a wild place like Polar Regions, deserts, tropical forests and read about the animals that live there. Check out the Remarkable Animals section and learn about some of earth's most unusual creatures. (+)

www.AN8.smork.com   www.panda.org/kids/wildlife

Five Grosser than Gross Animal Facts

1 Vultures will throw up their rotting dinners onto things that scare them.

2 Some bears form wads of plant matter in their bottoms during the winter. This keeps them from getting their dens dirty while they rest.

3 A sea star sticks its stomach out of its body to eat. Seal droppings are the favorite food of some sea stars.

4 Tiny creatures inside the termite's stomach help it digest wood. They also give the termite a lot of gas.

5 Cows spend nine hours a day chewing cud. That means they eat some grass, swallow it, throw it up and chew some more!

Courtesy of Saint Louis Zoo at www.stlzoo.org

Awesome Internet Sites for Kids

Nova Online—Wild Wolves

Ow…ooooo! Do you speak wolf? What does it mean when wild wolves howl? Listen and learn the language of wolves. Read an interview with a wolf expert to find out how wolves are making a come back or discover how dogs and wolves are related. (+)

www.AN9.smork.com www.pbs.org/wgbh/nova/wolves

Zooish.com

Zooish has it all. Animal pictures, animal info, even cartoon animals! Download pet toons or sea toons, read Amazing Animal Facts, or look at some great animal pictures. When you're done, play the Farm Quiz and see how you do. Way more animals here than in any zoo. (-/+)

www.AN10.smork.com www.zooish.com

Zoom Whales

Are whales fish or mammals? Do whales breathe under water? Are all whales huge? Zoom into Zoom Whales to find out all there is to know about this special mammal. Discover the differences between the many species like the Beluga Whale, Orca the killer whale, the Humpback Whale and more. (-/+)

www.AN11.smork.com
www.enchantedlearning.com/subjects/whales

Don't be fooled. When a bag, box or other paper item says that it is 100% recyclable that means that you can recycle it. It does not mean that it is made out of recycled paper. SMORK prints on 100% recycled paper.

zzArt Room

More than your typical arts and crafts site—visit the Art Room and learn how to think like an artist. The Art Room teaches you how to keep an artist's sketchbook and how to look at the world from different points of view. Smork enjoyed thinking and drawing like a cat. **(-/+)**
www.AC1.smork.com www.arts.ufl.edu/art/rt_room

Art Safari

Find adventure at New York's Museum of Modern Art. Look at cool animal paintings and sculptures. Write a story about what you think the artists want to say. Create your own computer-generated artwork. Your stories and pictures could be posted on the web. Now that's wild! **(-/+)**
www.AC2.smork.com
www.moma.org/onlineprojects/artsafari/index.html

Arthur's Art Studio (PBS)

Have fun with Arthur's little sister, D.W. Visit her art studio and paint right on the computer or print pictures of Arthur, Buster, Francine and the rest of the gang. D.W. will teach you how to draw Arthur step-by-step. Visit the Art Gallery and learn how your own artwork can be seen on the Web. **(-/+)**
www.AC3.smork.com
www.pbskids.org/arthur/games/artstudio

Arts Workshop: Children's Museum Of Indianapolis

Create your own multimedia production. You're in charge of the story, set, characters, music, and choreography. Invite your friends and family to see your production online. Learn about sculptures and sculptors and make your own sculptures at home with stuff you find around the house. **(-/+)**
www.AC4.smork.com
www.childrensmuseum.org/artsworkshop/index3.html

IMPORTANT TIP

It says you need to register first?

Sometimes when you register before you use a site, you'll end up getting all kinds of unwanted e-mail, and there are other safety concerns too.

Here are some tips before you register:

1. Check with an adult in your home to make sure it's o.k.

2. Check and see whether you can visit the site as a "guest". Sometimes, it only seems as if you must register first, but you don't really have to.

3. Be **very** careful about what information you give out when you register. You should not have to give your real name, address, or telephone number, to anybody, ever.

Not Sure? Ask an Adult in Your Home.

Coloring 4 Kids
You'll have a load of fun at this site with more than 500 games and art activities. Enjoy animated online print and paint, drawing, color-by-numbers, or e-cards. Pick one of many topics, including holidays, space exploration, dinosaurs, frogs, or disco nite. **(-/+)**
www.AC5.smork.com   www.coloringpage.org

coloring.com
This site is an online art book. Pick one of the many pictures and use your mouse as a crayon. There are lots of bright shades and patterns to choose from. You can register for a free account or just click onto the words and start. **(-/+)**
www.AC6.smork.com   www.coloring.com

Kaleidoscope Painter
Who can resist the thrill of looking through a kaleidoscope's magical eye? With kaleidoscope painter, you become the magician behind the changing mosaic. Create dazzling new patterns as you drip red, yellow, indigo, fuschia, green and other bright shades across a virtual canvas, then sit back and admire your art. **(-)**
www.AC7.smork.com
www.permadi.com/java/spaint/spaint.html

IMPORTANT TIP

Smork's Rules for Staying Safe Online

1 I will ALWAYS tell Mom, Dad or another adult if something is confusing, or seems scary, or threatening.

2 I will NEVER give out my full name, real address, telephone number, school name or location, or any other information which can identify me.

3 I will NEVER have a face-to-face meeting with someone I've met online.

4 I will NEVER respond online to any messages that use bad words or words that are scary, threatening, or just feel weird. If I get that kind of message, I will tell an adult immediately.

5 I will NEVER go into a new site or part of a site that is going to cost money without first asking permission from my parent or teacher.

6 I will NOT give out a credit card number online without a parent present.

Headbone Zone

This monitored chat zone offers a variety of topics, such as The Kids Room, The Teen Lounge, and The Price of Fame. Chats, open from 2–6pm (Pacific) weekdays and 10am–6pm on weekends are limited to 25 kids and are closely monitored by adults. Chatters are not allowed to give out personal info, swear or act rudely. (+)

www.CH1.smork.com www.headbone.com/friends/chat

Kidfu

At Kidfu, you rule because it's an online community especially for kids. Since the site is both cool and safe, parents are into it as well. Smork loved the note passer and the non-violent games. You'll need Flash for this site. (-/+)

www.CH2.smork.com www.kidfu.com

Ability Online

Find a friend and be a friend! Share your experiences, stories and interests. It doesn't matter what you look like or how you walk and talk, just let your personality shine through. Chat with friends online, find an e-mail pal or play some games together. Everyone is welcome here! (-/+)

www.CH3.smork.com www.ablelink.org

Kidsworld

Want to hangout with kids your age from all over the globe? Try Kidsworld, which calls itself "The Safest Worldwide Chat for Kids". Log on and discuss your thoughts, ideas, and dreams with lots of other kids. Remember to ask your parents before trying this or any other chat room. (+)

www.CH4.smork.com www.kidsworld.org

Free clip art from hundreds of different subjects

animals

mummys

...even aliens!

Clip art courtesy of Clips Ahoy at www.clipsahoy.com, and Awesome Clip art for Kids at www.awesomeclipartforkids.com.

Awesome Clip Art For Kids

Awesome Clip Art For Kids is awesome. What's cool about this site is that web host, Tom Brown, is 13 years old, so he knows what you like. Here, you can copy and paste animals, creatures, robots, toys or holiday art.

www.CL1.smork.com   www.awesomeclipartforkids.com

Discovery School's Clip Art Gallery

Need pictures? Discovery has them by the hundreds! If you need graphics for school, home, or fun, you'll find many to choose from at this hip clip art gallery, which includes animations. Choose from safety, social studies, language arts, fun and games, awards, science, math, music, sports, and technology. **(-/+)**

www.CL2.smork.com   www.school.discovery.com/clipart

Emma's Iguana Clip Art Page

Leapin' Lizards! Scaly critters are slithering everywhere at this cool site for hot iguana graphics. Emma has iguana heads, iguana buttons, and iguana backgrounds. You'll see iguanas sitting, sleeping, lying on computers, and begging for bread. Don't miss the rainbow iguana, or his friend made of veggies! **(-/+)**

www.CL3.smork.com   www.ettnet.se/~egils/ig-art.html

Kids Domain

Go crazy creating awesome web pages with loads of free icons from Kids Domain. Choose images from great categories like cartoons, games, dinosaurs, Star Wars, space, pets, animals, holidays, people, around the world, flowers, alphabets, bikes, boats, and trucks. **(-/+)**

www.CL4.smork.com   www.kidsdomain.com/clip

and for special events.

...like winter

Halloween

and New Years.

Clip art courtesy of Kids Domain at www.kidsdomain.com

Kidzpage.com

Have a field day picking from Kidzpage's 1200 free images. Choose buttons, backgrounds, bullets and accents, or photos. Use clip art to decorate your web page or to add illustrations to your school reports and projects. Choose from categories like characters, insects, sports, toys, fish, food, clowns, and art. (-/+)

www.CL5.smork.com   www.thekidzpage.com/freeclipart.htm

Three Bird Studios Clip Art

Use free folk art images "made by the people" to make and animate your own designs. These unique collections include dinosaurs, Christmas, cartoons, mythology, and Japanese crests. Download folk art from Africa, Mexico and the Orient or read "Ketchup", the tale of the boy who liked ketchup a lot! (-/+)

www.CL6.smork.com   www.countryfriends.org/KWClipArt.html

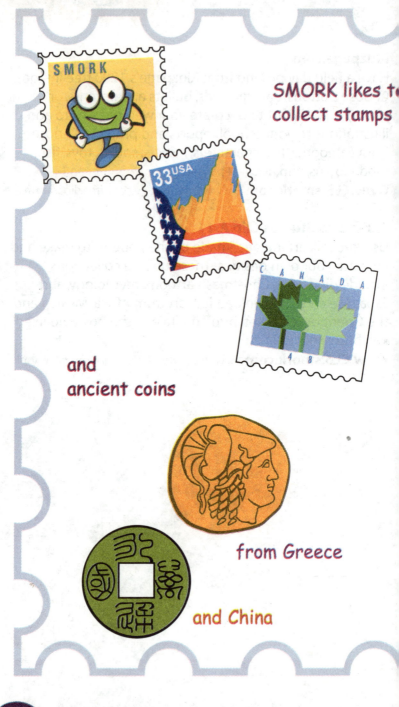

SMORK likes to collect stamps

and
ancient coins

from Greece

and China

BNAP Stamp Collecting for Kids

Try out a fun new hobby and take an adventure in stamp collecting at this colorful site. Get tips and ideas on how to get started, what to collect, trading, and stamp "conditions". Play stamp games and learn about stamps and collecting in Canada, the U.S., and the world. **(-/+)**

www.CO1.smork.com   www.bnaps.org/stamps4kids

H.I.P. Pocket Change—The U.S. Mint

Coins are like history in your pocket. Check out this site to discover the people who appear on U.S. coins and the people who use them. Visit Camp Coin to learn about collecting coins. See how coins are made, and play games such as "Making Change" and "Coin Memory Machine". **(-/+)**

www.CO2.smork.com   www.usmint.gov/kids

Smithsonian Kids Collecting

Become a treasure hunter! Choose stuff that is shiny or dull, small or big, plain or fancy. Collect coins, snow globes, miniatures, wind chimes, lunchboxes, cars, or anything you want. Learn how to start a collection, care for it, organize it and more. See Smithsonian's neat collections of rocks, minerals, stamps, and coins. **(-/+)**

www.CO3.smork.com   http://kids.si.edu/collecting

Fossils and Fossil Collecting

Imagine collecting things that are millions of years old! You can find fossils all over the place and the best part is—you don't have to pay for them. This site will tell you how fossils are formed, how to identify them and how look after them. So, dig in! **(+)**

www.CO4.smork.com   http://web.ukonline.co.uk/conker/fossils

Kids Can Make a Difference!

In Chelmsford, Massachusetts a twelve-year old started a petition and testified with friends at a town meeting to protect a wooded area from being destroyed by a condominium development project. The woods are still there.

A Chicago community health clinic that provides services for poor, pregnant women and infants was about to be shut down for lack of funds. Fifty children organized a protest in front of the clinic drawing the attention of the media and lawmakers. The clinic remained open.

Fourth Grade students in Kittery Maine ran a canned food drive at their school and donated the food to the local food pantry. Representatives of the classes helped prepare the food for distribution to the clients of the food pantry.

Facts courtesy of Kids Can Make a Difference at www.kids.maine.org/cando.htm

GreatKids Network

Kids make a difference! Read real-life stories of great kids who make outstanding contributions to our world. Why make the effort to help others? Check the Bulletin Board for answers from kids like you. Submit your own story and great kid photos. Smork likes the comic strip, "The Adventures of GreatKid Supreme".

www.CB1.smork.com www.greatkids.com

Kids and Community

How does a town become a community? Who decides where to put the sidewalks and playgrounds? How do you get people to visit a town called Dead Skunk Junction? At this site about city planning, create Crazy City Stories, paint "word pictures", or go on a Scavenger Hunt to collect things that tell a story about your hometown. (+)

www.CB2.smork.com www.planning.org/kidsandcommunity

Kids Care Clubs

Start a Kids Club in your community and join over 400 kids clubs in Canada and the USA. Kids Care will send you a club kit packed full of ideas on how kids in your community can help—locally and worldwide. Learn how to raise money, do good deeds, and make a big difference. Parents/Teachers must submit the registration form. (+)

www.CB3.smork.com www.kidscare.org/kidscare

Did You Know?

Dinosaurs used to rule the Earth during the Mesozoic Era or "The Age of the Reptiles". This era is divided into 3 periods:

Triassic   245–208 million years ago

Podokesaurus
very small with two legs and a long tail
Saltoposuchus
small, with a long tail, bipedal (standing on two legs)

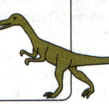

Podokesurus

Jurassic   145 million years ago

Camptosaurus
bipedal herbivores (vegetarian)
Stegosaurus
huge herbivore, covered with diamond-shaped bony plates rising along its back, with a small head, and spiny tail.

Stegosaurus

Cretaceous   145–60 million years ago

Edmontosaurus
duck-bills, herbivores, able to move on two or four legs, crests of various shapes and sizes on top of their heads.

Tyrannosaurus rex
the largest carnivore ever, a giant predator that overpowered anything it could catch, small forearms, taloned feet, great teeth.

T. Rex

Billy Bear 4 Kids Land O' Dinosaurs
Smork thinks his younger friends will find fun at this dino-mite site. Learn all about these huge creatures with information pages and flash cards. Play a dino dig memory game or connect the dino dots. Try the jigsaw puzzle or download dino fonts, screensavers, and other fun stuff. (-)
www.DN1.smork.com
www.billybear4kids.com/dinosaurs/long-long-ago.html

Discovering Dinosaurs
Dare to discover at this fantastic dinosaur site. "Adopt" your own T-Rex or play "What did your dino have for dinner?" See how scientific theories change over time and read about dinosaurs' environments, anatomy, behavior, and physiology. Learn the meanings of dinosaur root words or visit a dinosaur family tree. (+)
www.DN2.smork.com www.dinosaurs.eb.com/dinosaurs

Indianapolis Children's Museum Dinosphere
This site will take you on a wild adventure back to a time when huge, roaring beasts roamed the Earth. Learn about when dinosaurs lived, their names, what they ate, and how they talked. Find out how fossils form and how scientists dig them up. (+)
www.DN3.smork.com
http://tcm.childrensmuseum.org/dinosphere/index.htm

Zoom Dinosaurs
Zoom into Zoom Dinosaurs for everything from dinosaur behaviour, to fossils to reasons for extinction. Smork loved painting the Dinosaur Printouts, and catching up on the Dino News. There is even an illustrated Dinosaur Dictionary. How cool is that? (-/+)
www.DN4.smork.com
www.enchantedlearning.com/subjects/dinosaurs

Saving energy around your home:

Fight the light!

1. Turn the lights out before you leave a room.
2. When you know of a light that everyone forgets to turn off, make a sign to hang next to the switch that says "Lights Out!" or "Don't forget!"
3. Use compact fluorescent light bulbs. They produce the same amount of light by using $\frac{1}{4}$ of the electricity. Plus they last for years without burning out.

Don't leave things turned on

Turn off your computer, TV, radios or games that use electricity when you're not using them. Some devices, like modems or other networking boxes are drawing small amounts of power all the time. Check with your folks first, but the best thing to do is turn them ALL off.

Energy Information

Let the Energy Ant guide you through this site to increase your knowledge of energy. This excellent resource, which started as a school project, explains energy and energy sources in terms we can all understand. There are also short biographies about important people who contributed to the field. **(+)**

www.EG1.smork.com www.eia.doe.gov/kids

Energy Quest

Some of the energy we use is renewable—solar and wind, for example. Many of the most common types of energy we use are not renewable and everyone has to help ensure they don't run out. Find out about different kinds of energy and "Watt's New" in energy research. Learn what you can to do help save energy. **(-/+)**

www.EG2.smork.com www.energyquest.ca.gov

E-patrol

E-patrol lets you click onto different parts of a home for practical hints on how to save energy. Deciding what you want to eat before you open the refrigerator is one of the many ways that you can help preserve our resources. **(-/+)**

www.EG3.smork.com www.sprint.com/epatrol/ep-energy.html

The Power Lab

This site is so high energy that it's named The Power Lab. Find out about electric cars and the world's greatest energy heroes like Thomas Edison. You'll also find practical safety hints such as what to do when you get a piece of toast stuck in the toaster. **(-/+)**

www.EG4.smork.com www.edisonkids.com

SMORK is proud that Awesome Internet Sites is printed on 100% Recycled Paper. **

Whenever you can, SMORK asks you to show you care about our planet:

Please REDUCE the amount of stuff you use;

Please RE-USE things for as long as you can before buying replacements; and

Please RECYCLE everything that you can.

** Our paper is processed without chlorine, is made of 100% post-consumer content, and is Ancient Forest Friendly.

Canadian Botanical Conservation Network

This "KIDS ONLY" site teaches about plants, why they might disappear, and what you can do to help save them. Learn about bio-diversity, plant anatomy, "coneheads" and "alien invasions". Conduct your own plant experiments. Learn how to save the green stuff in your hometown. (+)

www.EV1.smork.com
www.rbg.ca/cbcn/en/kids/kidsindex.htm

CWS Kid's Zone

Oliver the loon represents the Kid's Zone on this Canadian Wildlife Services site. Click on the Games section for some cool environmental fun or visit Links for Projects to help you with your homework. This is your zone, so check it out! (+)

www.EV2.smork.com   www.cws-scf.ec.gc.ca/kids/index_e.cfm

Defenders Of Wildlife—Kids' Planet

Become a Wildlife Defender. Play some wild games and learn about animals that are on the endangered species list. The garden spider will be happy to explain the Web of Life for you; after all, he's an expert on webs. (+)

www.EV3.smork.com   www.kidsplanet.org

EPA—Student Center

A planet full of information at the click of a mouse. Use this giant directory to explore just about any environmental issue: Air, Conservation, Ecosystems, Human Health, Water and more. This is a great site to use for homework, science projects and research papers (+)

www.EV4.smork.com   www.epa.gov/students/index.html

Help Save Animals and their Habitats

1 Recycle everything you can: newspapers, cans, glass, aluminum foil and pans, egg cartons, etc.

2 Save your kitchen vegetable scraps for the compost pile—keep a small container on the kitchen counter to throw vegetable scraps into, and then empty it daily.

3 Do not use pesticides. Fly swatters work very well.

4 Clean your house with vinegar and water or baking soda instead of chemical products.

5 Use cold water instead of hot whenever you can. Save water and take short showers.

6 Use cloth rags and not paper towels, for cleaning up.

7 Don't leave water running needlessly.

8 Turn out the lights, fan or radio if you aren't in the room to enjoy them.

Courtesy of The Oregon Zoo at www.oregonzoo.org

Awesome Internet Sites for Kids

Especially For Kids—Oil Spills
What's the story on oil spills? How do plants and animals recover? You'll discover lots of facts, information and pictures. A great site for report writers, it includes experiments you can do at home, as demonstrations in class or even science fair projects. (-/+)
www.EV5.smork.com
www.response.restoration.noaa.gov/kids/kids.html

Exploring The Environment—K-4 Earth Science Modules
Learn about weather, seasons, climate and biomes. Play the Weather Game, an online quiz show, and test your knowledge about the weather. Pack a suitcase to test your knowledge about biomes, or create an online masterpiece. Games take a few minutes to load. (-/+)
www.EV6.smork.com
www.cotf.edu/ete/modules/k4/k4modules.html

GF Awesome
Go wacky wild learning about worldwide weather, how animals respond to climate change and what kids are doing to help the environment. Check out cool research, projects, and a glossary. View "cool natural pictures gallery" or try "crazy activities" like Carrot Pump or Cricket Thermometer. Great teacher spot, too! (+)
www.EV7.smork.com www.gfawesome.org

Just For Kids (Hurricanes)
Hurricane Harry is a helpful dude who will guide you through the way hurricanes work, how they are measured, how they change the weather and cause damage. Learn what to do if a hurricane is coming and how hurricanes are named. Can you find your name on the list? (+)
www.EV8.smork.com www.ns.ec.gc.ca/weather/hurricane/kids.html

RECYCLE

Kids Zone (Ozone)

This portion of the Kid's Zone is all about the ozone. Find out what the deal is by clicking onto the "What's going on up there?" link. You can also learn how the ozone guards the earth and how to protect yourself from the unhealthy side of sunshine. (+)

www.EV9.smork.com   www.ec.gc.ca/ozone/tockidzn.htm

National Wildlife Federation: Ranger Rick's Kid Zone

Read wacky wildlife stories, play Did You Know, or learn riddles to stump your parents. Take super cool virtual tours of water, wetlands, or endangered species. Try neat outside activities like tree tracings and attracting wild creatures to your backyard. Explore the fun Ranger Rick magazine at "stuff to read". (-/+)

www.EV10.smork.com   www.nwf.org/kids

US EPA's Explorer's Club

Do you want to make the Earth a cleaner place to live? Join the Planet Protectors Club, take an "Environaut's" mission to Earth or play Recycle City and other interactive story games to learn how you can protect the air, land and water. Learn about endangered plants and animals or explore the Chesapeake Bay ecosystem. (-/+)

www.EV11.smork.com   www.epa.gov/kids

Zoom Rainforests

Who knew that rainforests could be so much fun? This site maps out where rainforests are located and describes the plants, animals and the people who live there. The illustrated glossary and animal print outs are awesome. (-/+)

www.EV12.smork.com
www.enchantedlearning.com/subjects/rainforest

When you're e-mailing your friends, use your keyboard characters to create facial expressions or emotions to show them how you feel.

:-) Your basic happy-face, this little face means that you're saying something with a smile —maybe to show that you're joking, or just happy!

;-) This wink means you're kidding or teasing.

:-D Ha ha! You're laughing hard at something funny!

:-I Indifferent. It's like, well whatever. Either way is O.K.

|-O That O-pen mouth is yawning or snoring.

|-I Way beyond bored—asleep.

:-/ Skeptical. You're not so sure about that. In fact, you're pretty doubtful.

:-(A frown—uh oh, you're not happy about something....

>:-(Beyond frowning ... angry!

see pp. 48 & 126 for more emoticons.

Emotion icons courtesy of www.chirpingbird.com/netpets

CBC 4 Kids
What do you dream of doing? Take a walk in someone else's shoes and imagine what the future might hold for you! Grab some photos and music to create your own movie or add a chapter to a story. Read articles about other kids and voice your opinion about them. (+)
www.EZ1.smork.com   www.cbc4kids.ca

Midlink
This wonderful e-mag, for students by students, showcases "exemplary work from creative classrooms around the globe". Read an article or submit one. Learn about human rights, census counting, and the stock market. (+)
www.EZ2.smork.com   http://longwood.cs.ucf.edu/~MidLink

National Geographic for Kids!
This is the online edition of National Geographic's *Classroom Magazine*. Explore the earth's people, places, and creatures with kid-geared articles and bright pictures. Try Geo's cool links, quick flicks and games like Rocket Explorer or Panda Chow. Go on an Online Shark Safari Adventure or enter really cool just-for-kids contests. (+)
www.EZ3.smork.com
http://magma.nationalgeographic.com/ngforkids/0204

Owl Kids Online
Here you choose the link that's right for you depending on your age. *ChickaDEE Net* and *Wired Owl* both give you a glimpse of what each magazine features, along with other information and activities. Subscribe online to any one of these fantastic magazines including *Chirp* for pre-schoolers. (-/+)
www.EZ4.smork.com   www.owlkids.com

 **IMPORTANT TIP**

Did someone ask for your name, address, or phone number online?

Tell your parent or teacher right away and don't write back to that person until a parent or guardian knows what's going on.

Sports Illustrated for Kids
This online version of the popular magazine offers kids news, games, and e-cards. Read about fantasy sports or test your sports trivia knowledge. Kids can vote in a current poll and write letters to the editor. (+)
www.EZ5.smork.com   www.sikids.com

Time Magazine for Kids
Visit this site and you'll be a news know-it-all in no time. Click on the ticker to get the scoop on current events. Create your own magazine or take a virtual vacation. Check out the latest movies, music and books. Dig into some games, explore and get involved. (+)
www.EZ6.smork.com   www.timeforkids.com

Yes Mag
This e-zine version of *Yes Mag*, Canada's Science Magazine for Kids, is a must-visit for all science buffs. The articles are written in plain language so they're easy to understand. Find out the Cutting Edge in science and technology news. Meet kids in science. (-/+)
www.EZ7.smork.com   www.yesmag.bc.ca

Smithsonian Magazine's Kids' Castle
A site fit for a king …and a queen. From famous people and animals, to sports and science, you're sure to find some interesting articles to read here. Voice your opinion on the message boards or drop by the clubhouse to catch up on the latest news. (+)
www.EZ8.smork.com   www.kidscastle.si.edu

Famous People with Disablities

Chris Burke

played the character Corky on the television series, *Life Goes On.* He was the first person with Down syndrome to star in a weekly television series.

Tom Cruise

a famous Hollywood actor, battles dyslexia which is a learning disability that alters the way the brain processes written material.

Facts courtesy of The Center for Disability Information & Referral (CeDIR), website at www.iidc.indiana.edu/cedir/kidsweb/people.html

Albert Einstein: Image and Impact

The American Institute of Physics offers a simple and informative biography of Albert Einstein, a mathematical genius. This telling of Einstein's story goes far beyond E=MC2 and offers details on his early years, great works, world fame, public concerns, the nuclear age and more. Includes great photos and illustrations. (+)

www.FP1.smork.com   www.aip.org/history/einstein

Anne Frank Center

This well-crafted, info-packed site is a warm tribute to a most famous young lady. The spirit of Anne Frank fills the pages in excerpts from her diaries, a scrapbook of photographs, and other accounts of her short life. This site has many rich resources for both students and teachers. (+)

www.FP2.smork.com   www.annefrank.com

Biography.com

Students writing reports or surfing for fun will enjoy Biography.com. This site details the lives of the world's most famous folks with more than 25,000 concise and informative biographies. Also access message boards, top 10 bios, and a "born on this day" bio feature. (+)

www.FP3.smork.com   www.biography.com

Time.Com's The Most Important People of the 20th Century

Improve your "famous people I.Q." with this collection of biographies. Find well-known personalities such as Anne Frank, Albert Einstein, Princess Diana, the Kennedys, Walt Disney, and Rosa Parks. Choose from categories like Leaders & Revolutionaries, Artists & Entertainers, Scientists & Thinkers, and Person Of The Century. (+)

www.FP4.smork.com   www.time.com/time/time100

Famous People with Disablities

Terence Parkin

an Olympic swimmer, has never been able to hear a race starter's signal. Born deaf, Terence uses a strobe light similar to a camera flash to signal the beginning of the race.

Marla Runyan

represented the United States in the 1500 meter track event at the 2000 Olympics. She was the first legally blind athlete to compete in an Olympics.

Jim Abbott

a major league pitcher, has thrown a no-hitter and won Olympic gold in 1988. He is the only player in major league baseball who was born with one hand.

Facts courtesy of The Center for Disability Information & Referral (CeDIR), website at
www.iidc.indiana.edu/cedir/kidsweb/people.html

Zoom Explorers

If you want to know about the people who walked on the moon or sailed the oceans and then started settlements, then Zoom Explorers is the site for you. Check out the undersea explorers like Jacques Cousteau who introduced us to the beauty of the ocean. (+)

www.FP5.smork.com   www.enchantedlearning.com/explorers

Zoom Inventors and Inventions

Have you ever wondered who invented bubble gum, band-aides, or basketballs? What about crayons, chocolate chips or Coca-Cola? This site is for those of us who want to know about who invented what and when. You can search the online dictionary alphabetically, by country, subject or time period. (+)

www.FP6.smork.com   www.enchantedlearning.com/inventors

The King Center

Be a part of the great dream Martin Luther King, Jr. had for America. He fought for peace, equality and justice. Access this fascinating site to learn more about the wonderful changes he made with his life. Listen to his inspiring sermons or print them out for projects. (+)

www.FP7.smork.com   www.thekingcenter.com

TRAVEL GAMES

Word Association

This game is really simple and lots of fun. Pick someone to say any word, the person next to them should say the first thing that comes to mind.

Go around from person to person, saying the first thing that pops into your head and see where things go. It's really funny to hear some of the stuff your family will come up with.

The only time you need to stop and start over is when someone takes to long to say something or you are all laughing so hard that no one can talk! This game is great for quick-thinking practice and it encourages confidence and creativity.

Courtesy of Kids Travel Fun at www.kidstravelfun.com/games.html

4kids.org

At this "techKNOWLEDGEy" site, Earl the safe surfer will teach you web safety or help you find sites in categories like Creatures Features, Grab Bag, or The Lab. Log your comments at Speakout, take Kid Quest to test your web IQ, or Ask Amy web questions. Play interactive musical instruments. **(-/+)**
www.FG1.smork.com   www.4kids.org

Apple Corps

Be an apple or a veggie for the day with this fun dress-up game. An online version of Mr. Potato Head, pick a fruit or vegetable body and then add ears, feet, glasses, hats, and other fun stuff. **(-)**
www.FG2.smork.com
http://apple-corps.westnet.com/apple_corps.html

Cartoon Network

Activities, puzzles, music and stories starring Batman, Power Puff Girls, Scooby Doo, Bugs Bunny and other friends from Cartoon Network. Watch short cartoons or draw your own. Check out the Flintstones and get your official Loyal Order of Water Buffalo membership. Yabba Dabba Doo! **(-/+)**
www.FG3.smork.com   www.cartoonnetwork.com

Julia's Rainbow Corner

Click on the Fun & Games cloud at Julia's homepage, and you'll find lots of great activities. Count to 10, read words, or type. Be artistic. Decorate a part of the world, or a cake, or make your own picture. Create a scary creature face—just click on the parts and see it change. **(-)**
www.FG4.smork.comwww.juliasrainbowcorner.com

These emoticons will let your your friends know how you really feel!

:-& You can't get the words out the way you want to! You're tongue-tied.

:-@ Screaming. Another way to scream on-line is TO WRITE IN ALL CAPITAL LETTERS! AAAAAAAAARGH!!!!

:-C Oooooh, someone is really disappointed about something.

:'-(Oh dear, someone is crying.

:-O Uh-oh! I can't believe that happened!

:-X My lips are sealed! I won't tell anybody, I promise!

:-P Nyaaaah! Giving the person a "raspberry"!

}:-) This is a devilish, mischevious face ... look out!

O:-) This face, on the other hand, is angelic. Nice halo!

see pp. 38 & 126 for more emoticons.

Emotion icons courtesy of www.chirpingbird.com/netpets

Kid's Corner
Tour the Kid's Corner where you can play hangman on the computer, and check out other kids' artwork. Your Turn invites you to send in your stuff if you want to see your picture, story or poem on the net. **(-/+)**
www.FG5.smork.com http://kids.ot.com

Kids Fun Canada
Loonie and Toonie will help you find fun things to do here. Try the Brementown sing-a-long game, listen to characters' voices, remember their order as they sing, and you try to repeat the songs. You can read tales, too! **(-/+)**
www.FG6.smork.com www.kidsfuncanada.com

The Little Animals Activity Centre
Have fun with little animals. Read a story with a bear. Learn to play music with a fox. Laugh at funny jokes with Puzzlesnuff, the Porcupine. Or learn to add or subtract better by playing a numbers game with an owl named Count Hoot. **(-)**
www.FG7.smork.com
www.bbc.co.uk/education/laac/index.shtml

Long Island Kids
Homework helper will make afternoon doses of science, English, math, and social studies more fun. Visit the art gallery to view or add a picture. Try kids-only "forums" on poetry, sports, movies, and family. Read or write silly stories or one-liners. Download free software for kids. **(-/+)**
www.FG8.smork.com www.longislandkids.org

IMPORTANT TIP

What's in a name?

Don't use your real name—make up something fun and interesting that won't tell anybody who you really are.

MysteryNet's Kids Mysteries
Want to learn how to do magic tricks? It's simple at Mystery Net. Just read the easy-to-follow instructions and you can learn magic tricks to show your family and friends. After you've learned a few tricks, try writing your own mystery, or read mysteries written by other kids. (-/+)
www.FG9.smork.com http://kids.mysterynet.com/magic

NIEHS Kids Pages
At this site, the National Institute of Environmental Health Studies will entertain you for hours. While many of the activities focus on Health and Science, there are also a number of interactive and action games. Smork enjoyed bashing the toxic bugs most of all. (+)
www.FG10.smork.com www.niehs.nih.gov/kids/games.htm

Online Checkers
What could be more fun on a rainy afternoon than a cozy game of checkers between you and your computer? This online version of a great game is loads of fun for all age groups, and highly addictive. (-/+)
www.FG11.smork.com
www.darkfish.com/checkers/Checkers.html

Puzzle Factory
Click here for free games and puzzles. Play arcade classics such as Pacman. Test your skills with slider puzzles and memory games, or put together an online jigsaw puzzle. (-/+)
www.FG12.smork.com http://puzzlefactory.com

Awesome Internet Sites for Kids

Web Battleship

A strategy game you can play with your computer. It is the web version of the Battleship board game. Try to sink your computer's ships before the computer sinks yours! You will also find links to other web games. **(+)**

www.FG13.smork.com   www.head-crash.com/battle

Who DUNNIT?

Visit a crime scene and you get to be the crime solver. Try to figure out who dunnit in the Case of the Barefoot Burglar. See the suspects, compare their fingerprints, footprints and even tooth prints. Take crime solving lessons on the homepage before you click onto the crime scene. **(+)**

www.FG14.smork.com

www.cyberbee.com/whodunnit/crime.html

What is the independent state within the city of Rome?

—Vatican City. Vatican city was made an independent state by Treaty in 1929.

What train takes people from one country to another, travelling underground?

—The Chunnel trains take passengers to/from London and Paris

Which Sea doesn't support any life forms and is the lowest place (below sea level) on earth?

—The Dead Sea is 1300 feet (400 metres) below sea level, and supports no organic life other than a few microbes. The high salt levels let people float on top of the water easily too!

Which lakes form the largest freshwater lake group in the world?

—The 5 Great Lakes that border Canada and the U.S. (Erie, Huron, Michigan, Ontario, and Superior) cover 95,000 square miles (over 244,000 sq. kms).

The Atlas of Canada
See maps showing environment, people, history, climate, health and more. Zoom in and out to get details about a specific area. Find out where rare plants are, what parts of the country have the healthiest population, where resources are, and other interesting information about what is where in Canada.
www.GE1.smork.com   www.atlas.gc.ca

Canada's Aquatic Environments
This site is all about the plants and animals that live in Canada's oceans, rivers, lakes and wetlands. There is also information on how people affect and manage their aquatic environments. Although the site is Canadian, other countries including the U.S share similar habitats. (+)
www.GE2.smork.com   www.aquatic.uoguelph.ca

FEMA for Kids
Hurricanes, Earthquakes, Tornadoes and Floods are a few types of disasters that are caused by weather. Some only happen in certain parts of the world. Find out about what causes different disasters and what to do if one happens where you live. Learn how to keep your house safe, and even what to do with your pets. (-/+)
www.GE3.smork.com   www.fema.gov/kids

Frozen Toes
Come explore the Canadian Arctic and follow a 7000-km expedition across the Great White North. Read reports from the trail or submit your own adventure stories. Click on Arctic Studies to learn more about northern geography, history, culture, people and wildlife. Check out Den Masters and discover why bears hibernate in the winter months. (++)
www.GE4.smork.com   www.frozentoes.com

Geonet

Geonet is the ultimate U.S. geography challenge. Learn to think geographically; discover how we change the earth's landscape whenever we interact with the environment. High scores can earn you the rank of GeoAdvisor, GeoExpert or GeoChampion. If you start now, you could even end up on the high score list! **(+)**
www.GE5.smork.com   www.eduplace.com/geonet

Parks Canada—Virtual Tours

Go on a virtual trip to Canada's national parks. Just click a province, then choose a park. Click on Virtual Tour videos to see and hear a video description of the park, view photos, or check out links for more information. **(+)**
www.GE6.smork.com
www.parkscanada.pch.gc.ca/thesite/virtual_e.cfm

Where Is That?

Where Is That? Play this game "where your mind is your map". FunBrain.com provides the map; you name the country, state or capital. To begin, simply choose your level of difficulty and a location like Africa, Asia or the World. Play on your own or with a friend. **(+)**
www.GE7.smork.com   www.funbrain.com/where/index.html

World Fact Book—Yahooligans

The world is at your fingertips with The World Factbook, an online C.I.A. publication. This geography reference will give you important facts about countries for school projects. You can also view the maps and flags of 276 nations. **(+)**
www.GE8.smork.com
www.yahooligans.com/reference/factbook

Girl's World

This site is pretty and powerful. It is dedicated to girls and young women, and tackles relevant issues from boy troubles to cool careers. Since girls all over the world write the content, A Girl's World is on your wavelength. **(++)**
www.GP1.smork.com   www.agirlsworld.com

GIRL POWER at work!

A 17 year Canadian girl (from Dundas, Ontario) has found a compound that prevents the death of brain cells in laboratory tests. She was awarded a $30,000 scholarship.

Courtesy of www.cbc4kids.ca

Girl Power!

It's great to be a girl! Learn how to become a zoologist, hurricane tracker, oceanographer, computer animator and more. Check out Body Wise for advice on eating right and feeling fit. See what other girls are saying in Girl Speak or learn how to help a friend with a problem in You're Not Alone. (+)

www.GP2.smork.com www.girlpower.gov

Girl Tech

Check out this global girl community where girls from 85 different countries participate. Read about embarrassing moments, boy troubles, or women astronauts. Learn sign language, foreign languages or pig Latin. Don't miss girl poems, girl gadgets, or sports. Girl power is fun! (++)

www.GP3.smork.com www.girltech.com

Girls@Play

Girls@Play is a site about girls' athletic dreams and how to achieve them. Find out where to play, what to eat, and Who's On Her Game. Check out To The Max where you can learn training tips, injury advice and how to go for it. (++)

www.GP4.smork.com www.caaws.ca/girlsatplay

Girlstart

This refreshing e-zine puts brains before beauty and concerns itself with what you think. The well-written articles feature real life situations such as coping with braces, and women at work. Girlstart also offers book reviews, groovy movies, girl art, cool science and games. (++)

www.GP5.smork.com www.girlstart.com

First Among Equals

This site is dedicated to the public and private lives of Canadian leaders. If you ever dreamed of being the Prime Minister click onto The Path to Power to find out how other great people made it happen. **(+)**

www.GO1.smork.com   www.nlc-bnc.ca/2/9/index-e.html

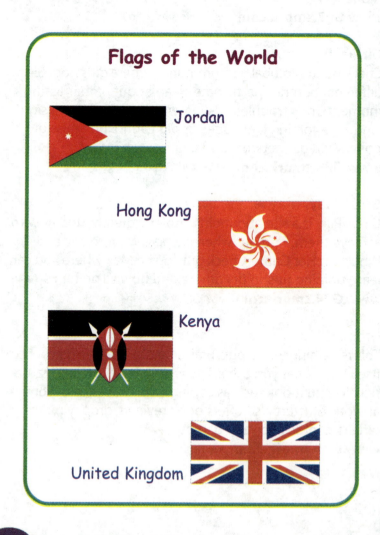

Flags of the World

Jordan

Hong Kong

Kenya

United Kingdom

King County Superior Court
This fun and informative site will help you understand
how the court system works and how criminals go to jail.
While this site outlines the U.S. court system, the process
is very similar to the criminal court system in Canada and
the U.K. (+)
www.GO2.smork.com   www.metrokc.gov/kcsc/kids

National Flags
Click on links to see colorful images of dozens of nations'
flags, from Argentina to Yugoslavia and many in between.
(-/+)
www.GO3.smork.com
http://155.187.10.12/flags/nation-flags.html

POTUS—Presidents of the U.S.
Hail to the chief! This useful resource offers everything you
ever wanted to know about the leaders of the United States.
Find background information, election results, cabinet
members, notable events, and interesting info on each
president. Access links to biographies, historical documents,
audio and video files, and other presidential sites. (+)
www.GO4.smork.com   http://ipl.si.umich.edu/div/potus

The Whitehouse
Who knew the Whitehouse could be so much fun? Check
out the history and current events, or find out what's up
with the president. Spotty, the family pet will take you on a
virtual tour of the Whitehouse, and explain everything
from a dog's viewpoint. (-/+)
www.GO5.smork.com   www.whitehouse.gov/kids

The ABC's of Vitamins

Vitamins are important substances found in our food that help our body grow and function properly.

Vitamin A
This vitamin is important for your vision and for healthy skin. You can get vitamin A from apricots, nectarines, cantaloupe, carrots, and spinach.

Vitamin B
This vitamin is important in metabolic activity. It helps your body produce and release energy. Fish like Tuna, whole wheat grains, spinach and broccoli are good sources of vitamin B.

Vitamin C
This vitamin is important for healthy gums and teeth, bones and muscles. It also helps your body fight against infections. You will find it in oranges, tangerines, lemon, grapefriut, strawberries, watermelon, and tomatoes.

theappleaday
This is a health website for kids. Find answers to your questions about, bad breath, wearing glasses, getting braces, how to stop bullies, yoga for kids and much more. There is even a great yucky list of weird foods that people from all over the world like to eat! **(-/+)**
www.HE1.smork.com www.student.city.ac.uk/~rc313

BBC Kid's Health
BBC seems to know everything and health is no exception. Learn how your body works, or play some creative mind games. This site explores the healthy balance of our heads and our limbs. Smork loved the interactive Body Tour. **(+)**
www.HE2.smork.com www.bbc.co.uk/health/kids

The FDA Kids' Home Page
This quick info site has many interesting facts. Learn how to make a safe home for your pet. Read all about vaccines and why we need them. Take a food safety quiz, do a word-find puzzle or help Mac & Molly inspect a warehouse. **(+)**
www.HE3.smork.com www.fda.gov/oc/opacom/kids

Kids Health
Calling All Kids! Got a homework assignment? This is the site you need. There is a huge glossary of medical words with easy definitions. Learn about staying healthy, everyday illnesses and injuries and dealing with feelings. Click on Watch Out to learn how to play safe indoors and out. **(+)**
www.HE4.smork.com www.kidshealth.org/kid

Bookmark Websites

Bookmarking gives you fast and easy access to websites you want to visit often without having to type in the web address each time you visit.

To bookmark sites:

In Microsoft Internet Explorer:

Most people have this one. If you aren't sure, read across the top of your screen. If you see an icon for "Favorites", you are in the right place.

1 Go to the site you want to bookmark.

2 From the pull-down **"Favorites"** menu, select **"Add to Favorites"**.

3 Click on the **"OK"** button.
That site will now appear on the bottom of your favorites list!

In Netscape Communicator:

1 Go to the site you want to bookmark.

2 Once there, from the Netscape pull-down **"Bookmarks"** menu, select **"Add Bookmark"**.
The site you picked should now appear at the end of your Netscape bookmarks list!

IMPORTANT TIP

When you pull down on "Favorites", the name of the site you are bookmarking will be shown. Sometimes, the name that shows isn't the name you want to save. Click in the box where the name shows, and type in a name that will help you remember what that site is.

Awesome Internet Sites for Kids

Kids Playground

Now you can play on the playground—even if it's raining outside. Choose from a mix-it-up game or a fast dash. You can send a friend a "jumbler" message and even help feed hungry kids around the world. So much fun, you will forget that you are learning about good health!

www.HE5.smork.com
www.kidshealthandfitness.com.au/index.html

Stay Alert Stay Safe

Stay Alert Stay Safe shows us how to watch out for trouble by being aware. Click onto the Booklet to help turn up your radar and create a safety plan at Central Control. Safety games and contests make this serious subject fun. **(-/+)**

www.HE6.smork.com   www.sass.ca

SGR4Kids

SGR4KIDS is a hip online e-zine that gives you cool reasons to be smoke-free. Learn what kids across the country think about smoking and what they're doing to ban it in their communities. Read what celebrities say about tobacco. Get real info about costs, health risks, ads aimed at kids, and more. **(+)**

www.HE7.smork.com
www.cdc.gov/tobacco/sgr/sgr4kids/sgrmenu.htm

Kids Help Phone

This groovy site gives info on how to deal with pressure, school, parents, sadness, friends, drugs, and other worries. Get confidential help from certified counselors or visit the online, self-serve library for facts and info. Share stories or offer encouragement at "Express Yourself." Vent your thoughts with "Letters Written Never Sent" or get advice to share with "Help Myself Help Others." **(-/+)**

www.HE8.smork.com   www.kidshelp.sympatico.ca/en

Did You Know?

On August 3, 1492, Columbus sailed with three ships who were called the *Pinta*, the *Niña*, and the *Santa Maria*. The crew of the *Pinta* was about 100, the crew of the *Niña* was about 50 and the crew of the *Santa Maria* was about 30 people.

After the difficult voyage that took about seventy days, they finally arrived at the American continent on October 12, 1492.

America's Story
This American Library site guides you through the history of the United States using pictures and simple language. Click on the map for a profile of each state, or meet some amazing Americans that have helped to shape the country. Here, you can have fun while you learn. **(+)**
www.HS1.smork.com
www.americaslibrary.gov/cgi-bin/page.cgi/es

Black History: Exploring African-American Issues on the Web
This site contains in-depth information on black history and includes topics often overlooked, such as buffalo soldiers, the Tuskagee Tragedy, the Little Rock Nine and church burnings. Read narratives or poetry, play an interactive treasure hunt game or participate in a video conference. Smork says, don't miss this great site! **(+)**
www.HS2.smork.com www.kn.pacbell.com/wired/BHM/AfroAm.html

Confederation for Kids
Learn Canada's story! This site tells how colonies once under British rule came together to form Canada, and how the country has grown since. Visit a gallery of neat photos or use the online glossary. Read about people involved in the Confederation, or learn more about Canadian provinces. Includes a teacher resource section. **(+)**
www.HS3.smork.com www.nlc-bnc.ca/2/2/index-e.html

Indian and Northern Affairs Canada—Kids' Stop
This fabulous site is all about Canada's Aboriginal people. Here you can discover Aboriginal history, language and people. The cool stuff section includes neat illustrations, monthly columns and an amazing description of National Aboriginal Day. Don't forget to celebrate June 21st.
www.HS4.smork.com www.ainc-inac.gc.ca/ks/english

Those Inventive Chinese

The Chinese take great pride in what is known as "the four inventions", the compass, gunpowder, paper and printing. They should be proud! These inventions transformed sea transport, warfare and literacy not just in China but all over the world.

What about spaghetti? If you think spaghetti is Italian, think again. Spaghetti originated in China. And the next time you are in a hardware store and pass a wheelbarrow, remind yourself that it was invented in China also.

Kids' Castle

Take a tour of Nottingham castle back in 1480. Click on a drawing of the Castle and surrounding grounds and choose the part you'd like to see. You can visit the Kitchens, the Great Hall, Lord Sherwood's Rooms, and even a jousting tournament. Each section has lots of information and activities to help you find out exactly what this English castle was like more than 500 years ago. (+)

www.HS5.smork.com   www.kotn.ntu.ac.uk/castle

National Women's Hall of Fame

Come and stand among great women and learn about the contributions American women have made in business, the arts, science and education. The database of in-depth biographies is organized alphabetically to simplify your search. (+)

www.HS6.smork.com   www.greatwomen.org

Prime Minister of Canada—Kid's Zone and Youth Pages

The Prime Minister offers young Canadians a thorough look into the government. Read the PM's biography, key initiatives or his message to kids. Learn facts about Canada and its government. The site includes teaching aids, Kids FAQs, quizzes, games, and a newsroom. (-/+)

www.HS7.smork.com
www.pm.gc.ca/default.asp?Language=E&Page=kidspage

The United States Holocaust Memorial Museum for Students

Maintained by the U.S. Holocaust Museum, this site offers a sobering look into the Holocaust's tragic events. Students can access an online library, exhibits, or collections and archives. Plan a visit to the museum, enter a writing and art contest, or simply browse around to learn more about this sad world tragedy. (+)

www.HS8.smork.com   www.ushmm.org/education/forstudents

DID YOU KNOW?

One of the most beautiful festivals in Thailand is Loy Krathong, a harvest festival celebrating the water's bounty. Loy Krathong takes place on the full moon in November.

Thais meet along the rivers edge with small wishing boats, called krathongs, made out of banana leaves and lit with candles and incense. They send their boats down the river with offerings of money and nuts to make up for any wrongdoings in the past year.

If their candles continue to burn until the krathong is out of sight, then their wish will come true!

123Baisakhi

Celebrate Baisakhi at Baisakhi.com. This site tells you about the customs and the significance of Baisakhki, a harvest festival, celebrated on April 13th in Northern India. Try out the recipes for traditional Punjabi dishes or send an animated Baisakhi e-card. (+)

www.HO1.smork.com   www.123baisakhi.com

Arbor Day—Carly's Kids corner

Arbor Day is a special day set aside to celebrate and plant trees. Learn why trees are important to our planet and our community. If there is no official Arbor Day where you live, pick a date and plant a tree! (+)

www.HO2.smork.com   www.arborday.org/carly

Birthday Party Ideas

Happy Birthday To You! Check out this site to organize the best party ever. Birthdaypartyideas.com offers great party themes that your friends will love. Safari, tea party and dress-up, are just a few. There's even a grown-up party section that you can share with your parents. (+)

www.HO3.smork.com   www.birthdaypartyideas.com

Black Dog's Holidays

It's never too early to start planning for the next holiday. Celebrate them all with Black Dog. He'll show you lots of things to see and do like great party games, crafts, e-cards, screensavers and more! Don't forget Mother's Day; learn how to tell Mom "I love you" in seven different languages. (-)

www.HO4.smork.com   http://www.blackdog.net/holiday.html

SING ALONG

The Twelve Days of Christmas

On the first day of Christmas,
my true love sent to me
A partridge in a pear tree.

On the second day of Christmas,
my true love sent to me
Two turtle doves,
And a partridge in a pear tree.

...Three French hens...
...Four calling birds...
...Five golden rings...
...Six geese a-laying...
...Seven swans a-swimming...
...Eight maids a-milking...
...Nine ladies dancing...
...Ten lords a-leaping...
...Eleven pipers piping...
...Twelve drummers drumming

Boo Did I Scare You?

While you can visit Boo Did I Scare You anytime of the year, this site is keen on Halloween. Play the Halloween Trick-or-Treat Safety game to make sure you know the deal. There are also other awesome Halloween links to choose from. **(-/+)**

www.HO5.smork.com
http://alphabet-soup.net/hall/halloween.html

Canada Day & General Canadian Activities

Come here for everything Canadian. Listen to the National Anthem. Print out some Canada Day pictures or send your friends a Canada Day e-card. There are also Canada Day puzzles, songs, crafts and more. About time, eh? **(-/+)**

www.HO6.smork.com www.dltk-kids.com/canada

Elle's Christmas Page

Ho, ho, ho! It's Christmas everyday at this festive site. Visit Christmas Village and send a letter to Santa, see the bakery, hear the choir singing or help decorate the town with trees, lights and Christmas decorations. Tour Elfland, listen to Christmas music, get recipes from Mrs. Claus, and play fun Christmas games. **(-/+)**

www.HO7.smork.com www.growley.com/main

Holidays on the Net

Learn about your favorite holidays and some you've never heard of. You'll find Passover, Easter, Qi Qiao Jie (Chinese Valentine's Day), Ramadan, Mardi Gras, Martin Luther King Jr. Day, Purim, Arbor Day, Kwanzaa, El Dia de Los Muertos, and more. Search for school project information, craft ideas, recipes, books and music. **(-/+)**

www.HO8.smork.com www.holidays.net

Kids Domain

You'll find plenty of reasons to celebrate here. With over 1,200 games, crafts and activities, you can have a party every day! Discover how countries across the world celebrate different holidays or create a great gift to surprise someone special any time of year. (-/+)

www.HO9.smork.com www.kidsdomain.com/holiday

Kid's Domain—Kwanzaa

Learn about Kwanzaa, a late-December African-American holiday celebrating the first crop harvest. Check out cool clip art and e-cards. Listen to drums, "The Music of Africa" and watch videos. Play games or make neat crafts like a family history book, a Fimo clay Kwanzaa candleholder, or a holiday shower curtain. (-/+)
www.HO10.smork.com
www.kidsdomain.com/holiday/kwanzaa

National Grandparents Day

This site is about the celebration of some very important people: grandparents. This site helps create a special project with a grandparent. Write an essay or a story about your grandparent's life, create a scrapbook, construct a family tree or videotape an interview. When you're done, invite your grandparent to school. (+)
www.HO11.smork.com   www.grandparents-day.net

Singing Songs of the Season

Listen to holiday tunes and read their lyrics at this delightful site. Enjoy classics such as "The Little Drummer Boy" and "Deck the Halls", or learn new ones like "Grandma Got Run Over by a Reindeer" and "Fred, Our Elf Hero". There's even a song in Spanish. (-/+)
www.HO12.smork.com   www.night.net/christmas/songs12.html-ssi

Torah Tots Holiday Fun and Games

This site is a celebration of Jewish holidays. Find out about fasting, new holidays, and traditional holidays like Chanukah, the festival of lights. Play Spin the Dreidel, read the story on Purim and check out Shavout, the holiday with many names. (-/+)
www.HO13.smork.com   www.torahtots.com/fungames.htm

What's Wrong?

There is one **incorrectly** spelled word in each group of four listed below. Can you find it?

1. a. lackadaisical
   b. hypochondriac
   c. philatalist
   d. counterfeit

2. a. prolifigate
   b. sycophant
   c. petulant
   d. millenium

3. a enforcable
   b. sabbatical
   c. emphysema
   d. interrogative

4. a. dawdle
   b. cacophony
   c. sacreligious
   d. articulate

Answers: **1c.** *philatalist* (philatelist); **2d.** *millenium* (millennium), **3a.** *enforcable* (enforceable); **4c.** *sacreligious* (sacrilegious)

Adapted from *GAMES Magazine: Big Book of Games*, edited by Ronnie Shushan, Workman Publishing, New York

BJ Pinchbeck's Homework Helper

BJ Pinchbeck, a teenage webmaster, provides you with a gateway to endless homework help. Click away for more than 700 links to sites that will help you with every school category, including "Recess." As BJ says, "If you can't find it here, then you just can't find it". (+)

www.HM1.smork.com
www.school.discovery.com/homeworkhelp/bjpinchbeck

Dictionary.com

With this dictionary at your fingertips, you'll have a fast way to look up words you need to know. Build your vocabulary by signing up for Word of the Day email. Check out links to Dr. Dictionary and Thesaurus.com or click Fun and Games for the daily crossword and word search puzzles. (+)

www.HM2.smork.com   www.dictionary.com

Eureka

This TV Ontario site is awesome, because you can ask a teacher for homework help in English or French. There are also several links to help you with literacy, math and science. Eureka is not just about the answer; it's about exploring solutions, and thinking problems through. (++)

www.HM3.smork.com   www.tvo.org/eureka

Fact Monster

The Fact Monster has gobbled up loads of information on topics ranging from world news to sports. Use this site to access timelines and maps, the almanac, the dictionary and the encyclopedia. Click on Homework Center for help in English, geography, history, math, science, and social studies. (+)

www.HM4.smork.com   www.factmonster.com

science

engl

math

compu

history

social

The Rudiments of Wisdom Encyclopaedia
If you're looking to add some spice to a project or just curious about almost everything there is to know, this site is nothing to sneeze at! You'll find thousands of fascinating facts complete with cartoons. You're sure to find a few laughs while you're clicking around. (+)
www.HM5.smork.com www.rudimentsofwisdom.com

Word Central
Get a hall pass and enter Word Central where you can find the correct spelling, definition and history of the words you need to know about. Visit the music room to compose a song. Want to be a mad scientist? Visit the science lab and run an English experiment. Who knows what you might come up with.
www.HM6.smork.com www.wordcentral.com

Kids Place
Boost your school skills, grades K-8, with these fun games and activities. Read with Gus the turtle, or learn skills to be a better test-taker. Try math brainteasers or language lessons in English and Spanish. Check out Power Proofreading and Science Library Adventures. Visit the fantastic Reading Scene for online, kids-only book clubs. (-/+)
www.HM7.smork.com www.eduplace.com/kids

Wonder Korner
Wonder Korner is "the question/answer place for curious kids". Get homework help by clicking on the yellow pencil. Try school tools, fun trivia, and author and illustrator info. Family Vacation Ideas has neat on-the-road recipes, camping songs and car games. Visit the unique Writer's Korner for tips, inspiration, and story ideas. (-/+)
www.HM8.smork.com www.peak.org/~bonwritr/wonder1.htm

Why did six run away from seven?

Because seven ate nine.

What did the snail say as it was riding on the turtle's back?

Wheee!

Why did the math book go to the doctor?

Because he had too many problems.

Why did the orange stop while crossing the road?

Because it ran out of juice.

Cantufind

Need more jokes? Cantufind is your Internet doorway to safe joke sites. If you like a good punch line, enjoy knock knock humor or simply want to make your friends groan, then this is the place for you. **(-/+)**

www.JO1.smork.com
http://cantufind.com/children_joke_sites.htm

CrazyBone

There are lots of jokes here. Read some, tell some to your friends, and send in some of your own. You can also learn magic tricks or play free games in six categories: puzzles, arcades, adventures, sports, aliens, and miscellaneous. Check out the tongue twisters, too. **(-/+)**

www.JO2.smork.com www.crazybone.com

Kidhumor

What's so funny? The thousands of jokes you'll find at this site. From silly and wacky, to pet humor to knock, knock jokes and more. You can also send a funny e-card, view audio clips, look at hilarious pictures or send in your own jokes. **(-/+)**

www.JO3.smork.com
http://kidhumor.glowport.com/links.html

laughLAB

SMORK liked laughLAB because it's not your regular joke site. This "science" experiment is about finding the funniest joke ever. The best part is that you can participate by rating jokes, or even submit your own. **(-/+)**

www.JO4.smork.com www.laughlab.co.uk/home

Why did the polar bear go to the south pole?
—Because he wanted to see his Aunt Arctica!

from Dawn (age 13), USA

What do you get when you cross a lawn and a kangaroo?
—a grasshopper!

from Laura (age 10), England

What do you get when you cross a snowman and a vampire?
—frostbite!

from Rhiannon (age 11), USA

What is a Koala's favourite drink?
—coca Koala!

from Harry (age 5), Australia

Kids' jokes courtesy of Wicked 4 kids at www.wicked4kids.com

Scatty.com
What a riot! Jokes, jokes and more jokes to tickle your funny bone. How many jokes would that be? Like over 12,000 of them. Knock-knock jokes, animal jokes, school jokes and much, much more. Tell them to your friends, little brothers and sisters, even Mom and Dad. (-/+)
www.JO5.smork.com   www.scatty.com

Wicked 4Kids
Jokes for kids by kids. Find loads of riddles, jokes, brainteasers, puzzles, and quizzes. Post your own jokes, play games or doodle your thoughts about music, books, school, pets and more on the Chat Boards. This site is cool or as they say in Australia—Wicked! (-/+)
www.JO6.smork.com   www.wicked4kids.com

Recycled, post consumer WHAT????

You are a consumer of paper. **Post** consumer means the paper comes from other paper that people have already used, and it's been recycled to be used again by you! That is the best choice in paper. Look for paper made from Post Consumer waste.

Illustration of Smork by Caroline Robinson, (age 8), Streams Elementary School, Pittsburgh, Pennsylvania.

Arts and Kids

Kid Power rules at this site for young artists. Enter the Arts and Kids art contest and have your work published on the Web. Play for hours in the virtual art gallery which shares the artwork of more than 30,000 kids. Try the daily puzzle contest or send a free e-card. **(-/+)**

www.4K1.smork.com   www.artsandkids.com

Global Story Train

Hop on the Global Story Train and read stories written and illustrated by kids from around the world. Ride the Magic Train, the Ghost Train, the Animal Train and others to find a topic that interests you. Check out the names, ages and countries of each Story Train contributor. **(-/+)**

www.4K2.smork.com   http://storytrain.kids-space.org

The Refrigerator

If your refrigerator at home is covered with drawings, then this is the site for you. The Refrigerator is an art contest which lets you participate in two ways: send in your own work for the competition or become an art critic and vote for the one you like best. **(-/+)**

www.4K3.smork.com   www.artcontest.com

Zuzu

Zuzu is an online magazine for and by kids just like you. What's really cool is that you can contribute your own stuff like art work, photos, short stories and poetry. Share your thoughts about your neighborhood, your collection or how to make the world a better place. **(+)**

www.4K4.smork.com   www.zuzu.org

Did you ever want to learn sign language?

K i d s

R u L e

American Sign Language Browser
Learn how to communicate in sign language. There are thousands of words and phrases at this easy-to-use site. Just click on a word and a video will pop up to show you how to move your hands. With a little practice, you'll get the hang of it in no time. (+)
www.LA1.smork.com
http://commtechlab.msu.edu/sites/aslweb/browser.htm

La Bamba Spanish Lessons
Grab your sombrero and sing along to popular Spanish songs like "La Bamba" and "La Cucaracha". Learn the alphabet and hundreds of different words in Spanish. You can print out some handy charts to practice common sentences. Don't miss the videos of Ricky Martin, Jennifer Lopez and Enrique Iglesias. (+)
www.LA2.smork.com
www.musicalspanish.com/samplechapter.htm

The French Language
This French language site will help you learn basic French or review some of the words you already know. The quizzes and print out activities cover all the important vocabulary like body parts, animals, numbers, and clothing. The English/French picture dictionary is fantastique! (-/+)
www.LA3.smork.com
www.enchantedlearning.com/themes/french.shtml

The Internet Picture Dictionary
If you're interested in how to say or spell a word in another language—this is an easy site to use. Choose from French, German, Italian, Spanish or English. Type in your word and select a language, or browse by letter or category. Challenge your memory with flashcards and word scrambles. (-/+)
www.LA4.smork.com   www.pdictionary.com

Awesome Internet Sites for Kids   87

prime numbers are numbers that have only two factors, like 2,3,5,7

a line is a straight path in a plane, extending in both directions with no end.

A fraction is a number that names part of a whole or part of a group.

Definitions courtesy of All Math at www.allmath.com

AAA Math

AAA Math will help you get an A in math from kindergarten to grade 8. Here, you can practice basic math by playing games and solving problems. The best part about this site is the simple explanations of math topics. **(-/+)**
www.MA1.smork.com   www.aaamath.com

All Math

Try out the online Flash Cards at this site to test your skills at adding, subtracting, multiplying and dividing. You can choose the level of questions, and All Math will keep track of how you do. For the real math genius in you, try to figure out one of the Magic Squares. **(+)**
www.MA2.smork.com   www.allmath.com

Ask Dr. Math

Everything you want to know about math and now can you ask. Find answers to questions about addition, subtraction, multiplication, division, geometry, math history and much more. There are puzzles and projects and word problems. If you can't find your answer here—then write to Dr Math. Your teachers will love this site too. **(-/+)**
www.MA3.smork.com   www.mathforum.org/dr.math

Cool Math

Unleash the math beast at this super cool site! Use the online calculators to figure out your age in dog years or the distance between airports. Don't miss the Fractal Gallery! There's tons of cool stuff you can do with math. Put your brain in a knot and explore away. **(+)**
www.MA4.smork.com   www.coolmath.com

Smork's Awesome Mathematical Game

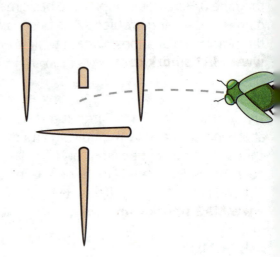

A Fly in My Soda Glass!

Arrange four toothpicks, as shown, to represent a soda glass, with a smaller tooth pick placed inside to represent a fly. The puzzle is to move just two sticks so that the glass is re-formed, but so that the fly—which may not be moved—winds up outside the glass. At the finish, the glass may be turned to the left or right, or even be upside down, but must be exactly the same shape as before.

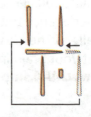

Answer: The arrows indicate which two matches move, and where.

Cool Math 4 Kids

Learning geometry, fractions and other math has never been so easy. Click here for simple explanations and pictures to help you understand. Play math games or find out if you can run your own business playing Lemonade Stand. When you think you're ready, take the Genius Test or try a few Mind Benders. (-/+)

www.MA5.smork.com www.coolmath4kids.com

Fleet Kids

This site is right on the money! Get down to business and learn how to manage your cash! Research the stock market, open a business or manage a baseball team. If you play the games right, you're bound to make a profit! (+)

www.MA6.smork.com www.fleetkids.com

Math Goodies

Mrs. Glosser shares her teaching and business experience in 400 pages of online math activities. This award-winning site features forums, newsletters, worksheets, lessons, and homework help. Math Goodies is a treat for students, parents and teachers as it helps us recognize the importance of math in the "real world". (+)

www.MA7.smork.com www.mathgoodies.com

The Math League

Here's math help for 4th through 8th graders! This site explains fractions, geometry, algebra, and more. You'll find plenty of examples, definitions, charts and graphs to help you gain confidence in solving mathematical problems. Your parents should also check out this site—so they can get it too! (+)

www.MA8.smork.com www.mathleague.com/help/help.htm

Smork Productions

4/7

Cinema

Have you ever wondered how movies are made? Write your own dialogue for a scene or put yourself in a producer's shoes by managing the production of a film. Learn how thousands of small details, and often hundreds of people, come together to create a Hollywood film. Three, two, one: Action! (+)

www.MO1.smork.com www.learner.org/exhibits/cinema

Cinemaniacs

You'll see stars when you register to become a Cinemaniac! (It's free but you'll need your parents' permission.) Access the latest movie news, enter competitions or take advantage of some amazing movie offers. Check out movie trailers and snoop around for the latest movie gossip. (+)

www.MO2.smork.com www.cinemaniacs.co.uk

Universal Kids

Universal Kids links to several popular movie sites so that you can visit the ones you like best online. Check out *Rocky and Bullwinkle*, *Land Before Time*, *The Flintstones in Viva Rock Vegas* and more. There's even an Artist's Den where you can paint much-loved characters like Babe. (-/+)

www.MO3.smork.com www.universalkids.com

Yahooligan's Movies

The Yahooligan movie site lets you check out video clips, and get the low down on the "now playing". Read reviews on upcoming films or visit past releases. Click here for ratings, release dates, pictures and names of cast and crew. (+)

www.MO4.smork.com www.yahooligans.com/content/movies

Alter Egos

Can you guess the musical artist from their nickname?

Who is "The King"?

Elvis Presley

What famous musical artist changed his name to a symbol?

Prince (The artist formerly known as Prince).

Who is the "Godfather of Soul"?

James Brown

A Guide to Medieval and Renaissance Instruments
You've probably heard of a Harp, a Bagpipe or a Flute, but do you know what sound a Lute makes? How about a Rackett or a Zinc? Visit this site to discover and hear the sounds of over 30 different Medieval musical instruments. Oldies but goodies. (+)
www.MU1.smork.com
www.s-hamilton.k12.ia.us/antiqua/instrumt.html

Campfire Songs from the MacScouter Scouting Resources Online
Gather around the campfire for this delightful collection of hard-to-find campfire tunes. You'll love this wagonload of gross songs (Smork's favorite…*Muff the Tragic Wagon*), good old campfire songs, silly songs, chants and songs for group leaders. (+)
www.MU2.smork.com   www.macscouter.com/Songs

Jazz Kids
This safe site from PBS helps kids discover the cool history behind jazz. With Now and Then, learn about jazz legends of yesterday and kid musicians of today. Try the Improvisation Station's jazz groove machine, a fun interactive jazz timeline from 1700–1960, or play Repeat the Beat.
www.MU3.smork.com   www.pbs.org/jazz/kids

Play Music
Play for hours at this delightful site. Send a musical e-card, meet composers and kid musicians, or play with musical cartoons. Learn about and listen to the orchestra's percussions, brass, and woodwinds. Create music, play in a virtual rhythm band, or learn how to make your own instrument at home. (-/+)
www.MU4.smork.com   www.playmusic.org

Instruments in an orchestra are divided into four groups:

Brass
> trumpets, horns, trombones, and tubas

Strings
> violin, viola, cello and bass

Percussion
> snare, bass, timpani, triangle, xylophone, and cymbals

Woodwinds
> flute, piccolo, oboe, english horn, clarinet, and bassoon

Playhouse Radio

Tune in to hundreds of great songs from all around the world on this cool online radio. Pick out tunes you like and build your very own CD. Read the lyrics and sing along or visit the workshop and learn how to make your own musical instruments. Don't miss the Treasure Hunt. (-)
www.MU5.smork.com http://www.playhouseradio.com

Songs for Scouts

Canada's Cottage Country Online has gathered the words to nearly one hundred songs to sing on the road, in the car, sitting around a campfire, or even in the shower. Find the lyrics to *Oh, Susana*, *Pop Goes the Weasel*, *Take Me Out to the BallGame* and dozens more. (+)
www.MU6.smork.com
www3.sympatico.ca/cottagecountry//dir-cam.htm#B

The Piano Education Page

Doh-re-me-fah … Sooooo, if you're looking for the key to hundreds of pages of information about the piano, this is the site for you! Get helpful tips and learn how to have fun with your lessons. Travel through time to meet a famous composer or pianist—and soooo much more! (+)
www.MU7.smork.com www.piano.avijon.com

"You know that children are growing up when they start asking questions that have answers."

—John J. Plomp

Crayola.com

Click here for inspiring activities for kids, parents and educators. Better than a brand new box of crayons, this site presents an ever changing pageant of arts and crafts ideas, games, fun facts, contests, book reviews and more. Teachers will find lesson plans, art techniques, creative writing projects, and science experiments.

www.PA1.smork.com www.crayola.com

Crayon Crawler

This is a downloadable kids-safe browser that prevents your child from accessing inappropriate content on the Internet. With Crayon Crawler, kids can only surf pre-approved web sites. For safe e-mail and chat, join Club Surf which provides a personal information filter and a language filter. Subscription fee required to join.

www.PA2.smork.com www.crayoncrawler.com

Family Education

This online magazine gives insight into your child's experiences at home, school, and play. Learn grade-specific advice, "must have" skills, the top signs of trouble, and how to identify possible learning disabilities. Get tips on kids and money, family issues, and how to deal with your child's first crush.

www.PA3.smork.com www.familyeducation.com

Frugal Moms

Keep your children happy without spending a small fortune. You'll find lots of entertaining ways to create something from nothing. Stir up some fun and easy recipes—like edible bugs, crayon cookies or rainbow Jello. Also find tips and strategies for saving money, chores, gardening, decorating and more.

www.PA4.smork.com   www.frugal-moms.com

Helping Your Child Learn Math

Make learning math a real and fun part of life. With chapters titled Math on the Go, Math in the Grocery Store, Math in the Home, and Math for the Fun of it, this site is full of activities you can do with your children. All activities provide a suggested grade level and easy to read instructions.

www.PA5.smork.com   www.ed.gov/pubs/parents/Math

Internet 101

If your children are light years ahead of you when it comes to accessing the Internet, this site will help you get up to speed. Learn about the origins of the World Wide Web, how the Internet works, browsers, email, downloads and lots more. Get hip to cyber lingo too.

www.PA6.smork.com   www.internet101.org

Kids Health

This site provides a reliable and practical source of health information about children. Offering up-to-date reports, articles and resources, you'll also find sections designed to help children and teens develop an understanding of many physical, emotional, and behavioral issues.

www.PA7.smork.com   www.kidshealth.org/parent

Movie Mom

All the information you need to choose movies for your 2-18 year olds. Movie Mom, Nell Minow, guides you through the best and worst of what's in theaters now, and gives her picks for best all time for theater and rentals. Movie Mom's five-check rating system makes for easy browsing.

www.PA8.smork.com www.moviemom.com

Net Nanny

This downloadable child safety software lets you view and edit the database of appropriate and objectionable sites. Net Nanny blocks both incoming and outgoing objectionable words and phrases. The Activity Log tracks the Web sites, newsgroups and chat rooms your kids visit and the information they send and receive.

www.PA9.smork.com www.netnanny.com/home/home.asp

Random House Kids

Know what your child is reading; check out this online home to all types of books including much-loved series books like the Magic Tree House, Dinotopia, Sammy Keyes Mysteries, and Junie B. Jones. You'll recognize popular titles and characters such as Arthur and Thomas the Tank Engine.

www.PA10.smork.com www.randomhouse.com/kids

Scholastic—Families

Scholastic's Family page "provides you with everything you need to encourage a love for learning". Select the right books for your child's age and development, and learn what to expect in school, including what's up with homework, developmental milestones, and what kids should know grade-by-grade.

www.PA11.smork.com www.scholastic.com/families

Streetplay.com
Remember stickball, handball, marbles and hopscotch? Those games that you played in the street, on the stoop, and against the wall, with balls, sticks, bottle caps or anything you could find? This site lists over 20 street games and rules. Teach your kids, reminisce and add your memories to the Stories page.
www.PA12.smork.com   www.streetplay.com/thegames

US Food and Drug Administration—Parents Corner
The Parents Corner covers a wide range of topics from juvenile diabetes to poison control. Find out how to give your child medicine, how to prevent dehydration, the latest news about the chicken pox vaccine and more.
www.PA13.smork.com
www.fda.gov/oc/opacom/kids/html/parents__corner.htm

> **Teaching kids to count is fine, but teaching them what counts is best.**
> —Bob Talbert

Zero to Three

From the National Center for Infants, Toddlers, and Families, this site offers endless resources and great info in digestible bites. Read an article on facing terrorism with kids, or learn about literacy, nutrition, childcare, physical development, and special needs of little ones.

www.PA14.smork.com   www.zerotothree.org

Big Chalk for Parents

Bigchalk.com is like a candy store for parents with rich resources on dozens of topics divided into age groups K–5, 6–8, or 9–12. Fun activities, business skills, women writers, current events, government, bullfighting, languages, arts and crafts, fitness, reference guides, and tutorials are some of the treats you'll sample here.

www.PA15.smork.com
www.bigchalk.com/cgi-bin/WebObjects/WOPortal.woa/db/Parents.html

Parent Soup

This resource center shares advice from parents and experts on topics such as banishing summer boredom, dealing with nagging children, and selecting an appropriate allowance. Track your child's development, find the meanings of names, and get tips on family pets and family travel. Click onto the parents' problem solver for help with specific troubles.

www.PA16.smork.com   www.parentsoup.com

4Kids2Play
Little ones will love this fun site. Play delightful click and drag games with virtual paper dolls, an animated circus, crazy zoo, music, playhouse, hedgehog, or little village. There are many puzzles, memory games, mazes, e-cards, and "brainwork," including Tic-tac-toe and Shuffle.
www.PR1.smork.com   www.4kids2play.nl/eng

Bob the Builder
Bob, Scoop, Muck, Dizzy and the rest of the construction crew are ready to play on your computer. Try fun, click-and-drag games. Help Bob tidy his tool shed, whack Farmer Pickles' spuds, or help Mrs. Percival teach spelling. Try viewing the site through a different country and/or language for more fun.
www.PR2.smork.com   www.bobthebuilder.org

Sesame Workshop
Full of fun and musical activities, this workshop is presented in the top style we've come to expect from the people at Sesame Street. Create your own opera or listen to sound bites in the Music Zone; keep busy at the Art Zone, or play in Elmo's World. Guaranteed to delight your preschooler.
www.PR3.smork.com   www.sesameworkshop.org

Tiny Planets
Meet the delightful duo, Bing and Bong, and their friends, the Flockers. These furry, white space creatures will take you for a ride on their space sofa. Travel to Tiny Planets where you can learn about health and friendship, how things work, music, how to help out, weather, nature, and more.
www.PR4.smork.com   www.tinyplanets.com

Wacky Words

Can you figure a familiar word, phrase, or proper name from each "wacky word"?

ScROLLS

MACKEREL

```
  e   e  eee eee
 eee  e  eee  e
eee  eee LIFE eee
eee  eee  e   e
 eee eee  e  eee
```

Answer from top to bottom: Dead Sea Scrolls, Holy mackerel, and Life of ease.

Adapted from *GAMES Magazine: Big Book of Games*, edited by Ronnie Shushan, Workman Publishing, New York

Aesop's Fables

At this site, you'll find the fables illustrated by art students. While the modern version of the fables makes them more real, the traditional ones are legendary. Be a smart tortoise and take your time here. (+)

www.RW1.smork.com   http://www.umass.edu/aesop

Alice in Wonderland: An Interactive Adventure

Be a Mad Hatter. Have fun with *Alice in Wonderland* poems, drawings and games. Play mad libs, concentration games, card tricks, or take Queen Anne's quiz. Ask the Caterpillar for advice, read *Jabberwocky*, put together the Humpty Dumpty puzzle, or send a Tweedledee E-postcard. (-/+)

www.RW2.smork.com
www.ruthannzaroff.com/wonderland/index.htm

Between The Lions

Get wild about reading! Learn how to read with a lion family. Just like on PBS, Leona and Lionel will take you on a reading adventure. Read with a Designated Reader, play interactive word games, listen to songs from the show, and print lots of stuff. (-)

www.RW3.smork.com   http://pbskids.org/lions

Dogmandu

Visit Lucky and read of his adventures as a dog trapped inside a boy's body. See lots of great pictures. This site, sponsored by 10 kids, helps lost animals at the Santa Monica animal shelter find homes and has links to other pet shelters. (-/+)

www.RW4.smork.com   www.members.aol.com/tenkids10

Elibs

Wacky adlib fans will flip for this fabulously fun site. Try the top 40 elibs in such categories as weird, poetry, school and scary. Don't miss the elibs poll, interactive group-written stories or the funkitizer, which translates your words with a Secret Decoder Ring into unique jibberish. **(+)**
www.RW5.smork.com   www.elibs.com

Giggle Poetry

Who knew that poetry could be this much fun? Giggle Poetry inspires your love of words through imaginative activities and contests. Chuckle at other kid's poetry or make up your own. "Roses are Red…" will never be the same! (-/+)
www.RW6.smork.com   www.gigglepoetry.com

Hiyah

Live happily ever after. Snuggle up and listen to fairy tales. Read-a-long or turn your speakers off to read on your own. There's a new story every week! (-)
www.RW7.smork.com   www.hiyah.com

Kidsbook

Want to be Mark Twain or Louisa May Alcott? Dr. Seuss or Shel Silverstein? Try writing your own story or poem and enter Browne's Funbooks writing contest. You can also read lots of writings by kids, ages 6–13. Take time to click through Browne's cool artwork and illustrations. (-/+)
www.RW8.smork.com
http://home.istar.ca/~kidsbook

KidNews.Com

Hang out for hours at this site that has stuff, for kids by kids, from all over the globe. Read topics like advice and opinions, kid news, sports, or reviews of books, websites, games, and movies. Submit creative writing for publication or find a pen pal. (+)
www.RW9.smork.com   www.kidnews.com

Awesome Internet Sites for Kids

Scholastic—Kids Fun Online

Kids just want to have fun, so log onto this site for a good time with characters like Harry Potter, Captain Underpants, Clifford, The Magic School Bus gang, Goosebumps and many more. Meet the authors and illustrators at their Scholastic web pages, play games, send e-cards and discover the newest book heroes. (-/+)

www.RW10.smork.com
www.scholastic.com/kids/home_flash.asp

Scholastic—Writers on Writing

Are you a poet, or a reporter? Do you dream up stories with dragons and flying carpets and magic beans? Learn how to write poetry, news stories, myths, book reports, mysteries, or fairytales from real writers in step-by-step workshops. Post questions about writing, publish your story online and receive a certificate of achievement. **(+)**

www.RW11.smork.com http://teacher.scholastic.com/writewit

Story Place

Visit Story Place and read a story that you help create. Click on a tale, then pick the names for all the players—the hero, the villain, even the town. See, hear and read the story after you've picked the names. You'll also find fun reading games and activities here. **(-)**

www.RW12.smork.com www.storyplace.org

Storyteller

Become an author. This site gives you great story ideas like "Your most embarrassing moment…", "My first day at Hogwart's school…", "As I walked into the cave...", and more. Just type in your story and press Publish My Story, or read over 11,000 stories by kids from around the world. **(-/+)**

www.RW13.smork.com
www.edbydesign.com/storyteller/index.html

The Magic Tree House

The Magic Tree House is a special place with a story of its own. Here you can ask the author questions or visit Magic Tree House book lists. The Readers and Writers Club guides you through creative story writing complete with characters, setting and a plot. **(+)**

www.RW14.smork.com
www.randomhouse.com/kids/magictreehouse/home.html

Captain Olin's Odyssey
Join Captain Olin's crazy crew for the space adventure of your life. Face problems of survival aboard the Star Ship Destiny. Learn about Mother Earth, water supply, garbage disposal, chemicals, clean air and safe packaging with tours like Not a Drop to Drink and Garbage in Doesn't Mean Garbage Out. (+)
www.SV1.smork.com   www.kcpt.org/olin

6 Top Actions to Make the World a Better Place

1 Buy Less Stuff

2 Buy Products From Socially Responsible Companies

3 Make Time for Loved Ones

4 Conserve Energy And Water

5 Watch Less TV

6 Join an Organization You Care About

Adapted from *The Better World Handbook*, by Ellis Jones, Ross Haenfler, and Brett Johnson, with Brian Klocke—www.betterworldhandbook.com

Awesome Internet Sites for Kids

Learning for a Sustainable Future
Travel with Sally and Billy on the Green Adventure to learn how to help the environment. Check out the International Youth Magazine's sections on environment, society, economy, take action and online activities. Your teachers can visit the center for online and classroom activities. (+)
www.SV2.smork.com   www.schoolnet.ca/learning

Planetpals.com
At Planetpals.com everyday is Earth Day. Each of the Planet Pal characters has a special rhyme to teach you how to be friendlier to our environment. Check out the pre-cycle section to find out what to do before the recycle stage. Be a pal and get involved. (-/+)
www.SV3.smork.com   www.planetpals.com

Planet Energy
The renewable energy trail teaches about types of energy that never run out, like solar, wind, water, and even waste. Find out what people all across the world are doing to solve energy shortages. You'll see neat pictures, graphics, and trivia. Finish your journey with fun energy games. (-/+)
www.SV4.smork.com   www.dti.gov.uk/renewable/ed_pack

Roofus' Solar and Efficient Neighborhood
Tour Roofus' Solar home to find out how you can make a difference by preserving energy. Learn how the sun can act as a natural energy source on your roof, in your garage, and in your own backyard. (-/+)
www.SV5.smork.com   www.eren.doe.gov/roofus

Science Twisters

Snowballs

Who can resist a good snowball fight? Snowballs are hardest to make when the temperature is

    a. right around freezing (32°F or 0°C)
    b. between 10° and 32°F (-12° and 0°C)
    c. below 10° F (-12°C)

c. To make a snowball you apply pressure with your hands, which melts enough ice to produce a layer of water between the snowflakes. With the pressure removed, the flakes stick together because the water forms a cohesive bond that is reinforced by the refreezing water. When the temperature is very low, the pressure required to melt the ice is too great to be exerted with the hands.

Ring around the moon

If the weather has been clear, a ring around the moon predicts:

    a. rain
    b. clear weather
    c. neither—the presence of the ring has nothing to do with the weather

a. Ice crystals form in high-altitude cirrus clouds that precede a rain front. These crystals refract light from the moon and give the appearance of a ring.

Adapted from *GAMES Magazine*: *Big Book of Games*, edited by Ronnie Shushan, Workman Publishing, New York

Alien Explorer
This site has lots of information on ecology, ponds and mammals. It shows you how to draw an alien or create one using paper maché. Click onto the free clipart section to download pictures that are out of this world. (+)
www.SC1.smork.com   www.alienexplorer.com

Astronomy for Kids
Easy to understand answers to out-of-this-world questions. This site is your guide to the sky, the planets and the stars. Don't forget to send a postcard, visit the puzzle page or explore Sky Links. (-/+)
www.SC2.smork.com   www.dustbunny.com/afk

Canadian Space Agency—Kidspace
Hey! What's up? Get your head out of the clouds and check out some funny space stuff. Discover experiments performed on missions, how robots are used and what astronauts eat. Touch down at the Cosmic Playground. You'll split your space suit laughing over "The Galaxy Song!"
www.SC3.smork.com   www.space.gc.ca/kidspace

The Constellations and Their Stars
What are constellations and where did they come from? What is Pegasus and Orion's Belt? And what about the Milky Way? This site will answers these questions and many more about the stars. Check out the Star Charts and Star Myths of the Greeks and Romans and the Astronomy Picture of the Day. (+)
www.SC4.smork.com
www.astro.wisc.edu/~dolan/constellations

DID YOU KNOW?

Nuclear materials are used for many other things besides nuclear power:

In nuclear medicine, to detect and treat certain illnesses.

To perform research at universities.

In industry, to locate cracks in steel and eliminate dust from film and compact discs.

To measure the amount of glue on a postage stamp and the amount of air whipped into ice cream.

Earth and Moon Viewer

For an out-of-this world view of the Earth, tune into the groovy Earth and Moon Viewer. See live satellite pictures of the Earth from the Sun, the Moon or the Earth's night side. View weather and cloud cover maps. Don't forget to check out the magical Moon, too. (+)

www.SC5.smork.com www.fourmilab.ch/earthview

Enchanted Learning—The Earth

Hey Earthlings. Why is the sky blue? Why are the oceans salty? What is the Greenhouse Effect? Find the answers to these earthly questions and more at this Enchanted Learning site about the Earth. Find simple explanations, pictures, graphs, and printable maps. A must see for school reports! (+)

www.SC6.smork.com
www.enchantedlearning.com/subjects/astronomy/planets/earth

Science Projects

Click here for super cool project ideas. Find out how much energy is in a peanut, make your own mini-lightning bolts, build a solar-powered hotdog cooker, or learn about the greenhouse effect by studying a car baking in the sun. Check first with your teacher or parent, as some activities require adult help. (+)

www.SC7.smork.com
www.energyquest.ca.gov/projects/index.html

Ethan's Solar Oven

Budding scientists will enjoy this e-journey through Ethan's science project, a working solar oven. Ethan gives details and walks viewers through research, variables, graphs, hypotheses and the conclusion to his experiment. (+)

www.SC8.smork.com
www.ethansolaroven.homestead.com/indexethansolaroven.html

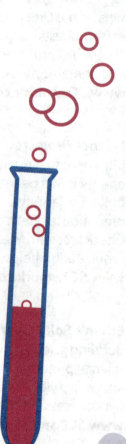

History of the Universe

This site tells the history behind our universe starting 15 billion years ago. Learn about the stars, atoms, fish, flowers, people, and the future. The language is advanced and the story complex, but the graphics and illustrations help to spark the interest of young readers. (+)
www.SC9.smork.com   www.historyoftheuniverse.com

Human Anatomy Online

Here the human body is subject to your examination. View images ranging from intestines to dental fillings, or watch animated clips of your bodily functions. Click on Descriptions for detailed explanations of muscles, bones and more. (++)
www.SC10.smork.com   www.innerbody.com

The Yuckiest Site on the Internet

This site delivers what it promises: lots of gross but interesting scientific facts. Here roaches rule, worms rock and our least pleasant bodily functions are openly discussed. Wendell the worm, the site's host, will answer the yuckiest of questions. (+)
www.SC11.smork.com   http://yucky.kids.discovery.com

Insecta Inspecta World

Bugs, bugs and more bugs. Beetles, butterflies, and bees. Explore the world of insects and how they live with us and around us. Find out about bugs in the news, bugs on money and bugs in art. Although this site uses some big words, the scientific terms are well explained. (++)
www.SC12.smork.com   www.insecta-inspecta.com

Science Twisters

Jumping Fleas

Some fleas can jump more than a foot—a 100 times their length. If we could jump as far in proportion to our height, we'd be clearing 50-story buildings. Why can't we?

a. A flea's legs, unlike a human's, are well-designed for jumping, since they are anatomically similar to catapults.

b. A human's larger body encounters too much air resistance.

c. With increasing size, the weight of an animal increases much faster than its strength.

c. An animal's weight varies according to the cube of its volume, its strength according to the square of its muscle-and-bone cross section. A human's strength relative to his size and weight therefore keeps him earthbound. If a flea's size were increased a thousandfold, its weight would be a billion times greater but its strength only a million times greater. The poor thing would be crushed by it's own weight.

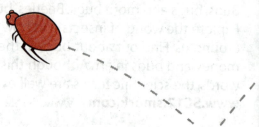

Adapted from *GAMES Magazine: Big Book of Games*, edited by Ronnie Shushan, Workman Publishing, New York

Journey North

This global study of wildlife migration teaches about the migrations of the earth's creatures. Students from the U.S. and Canada participate in this online, interactive science classroom. Track spring's progress as birds move, frogs reappear and flowers bloom. Read reports of Journey North Kids or post your own spring sighting. (+)

www.SC13.smork.com   www.learner.org/jnorth

NASA Kids

NASA Kids has super info on rockets and airplanes, astronauts living in space and great pictures of the planets. Do projects and play games or check out other kids' talent in the Creation Station. This site has all you need for a great space project. (+)

www.SC14.smork.com   http://kids.msfc.nasa.gov

Neurology for Kids

Have a zany brainy time with neurology (the study of the brain) at this super site. Learn all about your nervous system, brain basics, reflexes, senses, and neuroscientists. Try the fun online books, neat audio files, neuro worksheets and creative writing activities. Smork really likes the brain songs! (-/+)

www.SC15.smork.com
http://faculty.washington.edu/chudler/neurok.html

The Nine Planets

With the help of the space program, Bill Arnett brings the Solar System to your computer screen. Check out the photographs of the planets and the moons, and learn about their history and mythology. This is your universe! (+)

www.SC16.smork.com   www.nineplanets.org

Nye Labs

Bill Nye the "Science guy" demonstrates how to do science experiments, like tornado in a bottle. Click onto Unyeverse for a scientific memo, or check out the Episode Guides for the 411 on everything from germs to space exploration. Smork loved the extra terrestrial e-cards, and the great sound effects. (+)

www.SC17.smork.com   www.nyelabs.com

Willow

Oak

Maple

Poplar

Sycamore

Pond Dipping—Wildlife Ponds
Take a dip on the wild side. Learn about pond wildlife like frogs and toads, tadpoles, dragon flies, nymphs, pond bugs and other creatures. Want to see these wet critters in person? Go for a pond dip. Click here to find out how to do it safely. (+)
www.SC18.smork.com
http://web.ukonline.co.uk/conker/pond-dip

Space Daily
Space Daily is an online newspaper and your gateway to space. Here you can find out the latest space news from countries all over the world. Regular features include: Spacewar, Rocket Science, Launch Pad and Mars Daily. This site is great for school reports. (++)
www.SC19.smork.com   www.space.com

Windows to the Universe
Blast off to outer space and learn facts and myths about the skies and stars, Earth, Jupiter, and other planets. Learn about people who do space work, or ask scientists questions. Try games, puzzles, and workbooks. Send your buddies planet postcards, find ideas for school projects, or visit the By Kids space art museum. (+)
www.SC20.smork.com   www.windows.ucar.edu

The Wonderful World of Trees
Learn all about our tall, green and leafy friends. This site describes types of trees, what happens to them in ice storms, how you can help save trees, and the many ways we use them. Try games, puzzles, experiments, and a glossary. Peek into the tree family photo album. (-/+)
www.SC21.smork.com
www.domtar.com/arbre/english/start.htm

Common Baseball Superstitions

Spitting into your hand before picking up the bat brings good luck

A wad of gum stuck on a player's hat brings good luck.

It is bad luck if a dog walks across the diamond before the first pitch.

It is good luck to step on one of the bases before running off the field at the end of an inning.

It is bad luck to touch the baselines while running off and onto the field between innings.

Lending a bat to a fellow player is a serious jinx.

Some players will sleep with their bat to break out of a hitting slump or stay in a groove.

If a pitcher is throwing a perfect game or a no-hitter, never mention it while it's going on.

Facts courtesy of Fact Monster, website at www.factmonster.com

Black Belt Kids
Learn about the origins and styles of martial arts, karate kids, weapons, helpful books, and where to find dojo schools. Read "When I Was Your Age" stories from karate masters. Meet the man behind the martial arts magic of Mortal Kombat and The Teenage Mutant Ninja Turtles. (+)
www.SP1.smork.com   www.blackbeltmag.com/bbkids

Exploratorium: The Science of Hockey
If you're the type of person who needs to know EVERYTHING about hockey, join the San Jose Sharks at their Science of Hockey site. Find out the difference between fast ice and slow ice. Learn about new equipment and materials. Discover the tricks of hockey fitness, and lots more. (+)
www.SP2.smork.com   www.exploratorium.edu/hockey

Fact Monster—Sports
Gear yourself up for some little-known facts and superstitions about sports. Take a shot at Power Football or step up to the bat for Math Baseball. Read up on some animal athletes, Olympic news and the Boston Marathon. Be sure to check out the archives for endless reports on sports. (+)
www.SP3.smork.com   www.factmonster.com/sports.html

National Football League
The official NFL site for kids scores big with fun info and activities. Learn basic game rules, get an inside look at playing or working for the NFL, or check out statistics, scores, and standings. Play groovy games like Tackleman and Trainer Terror. Vote in a poll or watch highlights of the week. (+)
www.SP4.smork.com   www.playfootball.com

Sometimes emoticons describe things other than emotions, like what a person looks like or what they're doing:

B-) I wear glasses.

:-# This emoticon wears braces.

[:-) Can't tear him or herself away from the music—wearing a Walkman.

:-{) This is a guy with a mustache.

:-)= This guy wears a beard.

:-)> This is a guy with a goatee.

8-) Cool cat, wearing sunglasses, man.

8:-) Casually wearing sunglasses on your head.

(-: A left-handed e-mailer.

%-) This is what happens when you spend too much time in front of the computer. You get googly-eyed! Go outside and play!

see pp. 38 & 48 for more emoticons.

Emotion icons courtesy of www.chirpingbird.com/netpets

National Hockey League Kids

Hockey rules at this kids-only site. Check out features on players, fact sheets, bios, and photos. Read a hockey expert's answers to trivia questions from kids like you. Visit the league milestones, NHL calendar, and player birthdays. Join in games like Goal 2 Goal and Puck Blaster. **(+)**
www.SP5.smork.com   www.nhl.com/kids

SportsID.Com

Learn to catch a wave from surfing masters or let soccer pros teach you moves at this sporty spot. Choose from more than 1,500 video clips to learn basic or advanced skills in just about any sport you can imagine, including baseball, cycling, snowboarding, kayaking, and windsurfing. **(+)**
www.SP6.smork.com   www.sportsid.com

Women in Sports

Get the score on women in sports! Dive into hundreds of biographies and articles to find out what it takes to compete and be part of a team. From Archery to Weightlifting, you'll be impressed with the focus and strength of these talented, female athletes. A winning site for projects! **(+)**
www.SP7.smork.com   www.makeithappen.com/wis

> **Why isn't this paper bright white?**
> Paper companies sometimes use chlorine to bleach paper white. Using chlorine can be harmful to the environment. Smork's paper is chlorine free. **THIS IS WHAT PAPER SHOULD LOOK LIKE!**

Awesome Internet Sites for Kids

"The whole art of teaching is only
the art of awakening the natural
curiosity of young minds for
the purpose of satisfying it afterwards."

-Anatole France

**Illustrations by Josie Cuzzaniti,
Teacher, Toronto, ON, Canada.**

123Child.com

A virtual community for preschool teachers; find more than 1250 activities for young children in art, math, science, games, songs, dramatic play, and more. Share questions and answers, read about timely topics, or post comments on the bulletin board.

www.TE1.smork.com   www.123child.com

The Bridge: Oceans Science Teacher Resource Center

Dive into this endless array of ocean-science resources and lesson plans. Topics include aquaculture, policy, conservation, recreation, seafood, and more. Go on a virtual underwater expedition, Ask an Oceanographer, join The Troll Patrol, or sign up for Scuttlebutt, a marine educator's forum to exchange ideas and questions.

www.TE2.smork.com   www.vims.edu/bridge

Cells Alive

The cellular world comes to life at this informative site. You'll appreciate the clear explanations, the colorful graphics and the video clip options. The quizzes on cell structure, microbes, and the immune system are particularly useful.

www.TE3.smork.com   www.cellsalive.com

Debbie's Unit Factory—Remembrance Day

Debbie's Unit Factory provides links to Remembrance Day sites to develop lesson plans for this important Canadian Holiday. Find great material about Canadian war heroes, John McCrae's poem *In Flanders Fields*, and Bryan Adams' song, *Remembrance Day*. Teach the importance of Remembrance Day and how the poppy became its symbol.

www.TE4.smork.com   www.themeunits.com

Discovery School for Teachers

There's a lot to be discovered here! Create and store your customized lesson plans and generate work sheets or puzzles for almost any subject. You can access over 2,000 up-to-date education links and a large variety of clip art to dress up your handouts.

www.TE5.smork.com   http://school.discovery.com/teachers

Education World

"The Educator's Best Friend", this site is not only a search engine for educational Web sites, it also provides practical information for educators, information on how to integrate technology in the classroom, and articles written by education experts. Check out Lesson Planning, Curriculum Now, School Issues and Administrator's Desk.

www.TE6.smork.com   www.educationworld.com

Holidays on the Net

This great site will help you create extraordinary holiday lesson plans for students of all ages. You'll find activities, cards, crafts, pictures, books, music, and videos. Featured holidays include: Passover, Qi Qiao Jie (Chinese Valentine's Day), Ramadan, Mardi Gras, Martin Luther King, Jr. Day, Purim, Arbor Day, Kwanzaa, El Dia de Los Muertos.

www.TE7.smork.com   www.holidays.net

Insectclopedia

Insectclopedia is an excellent teacher resource for all aspects of the insect world. Your students will love the photographs of these creepy crawlies, and you'll be impressed by the wealth of information. The link to Grade Pal makes grading and tracking easy. Handouts and Lesson Plans are also available.

www.TE8.smork.com   www.insectclopedia.com

Teachers

This easy-to-navigate site has numerous resources for K-12 teachers including supplies, lesson plans, a searchable library with reference links and a vast database of teacher-contributed lesson plans. There are numerous chat boards and online meetings and workshops. Find informative columns and articles penned by various education professionals.

www.TE9.smork.com   www.teachers.net

Teacher Vision

The site features a huge lesson plan database, and a massive resource center. Click on myschoolonline to learn how to build a classroom web page. Check out Classroom Management and read about new techniques to enhance your classroom atmosphere. Visit Professional Development to keep certified and up-to-date on the latest teaching trends.

www.TE10.smork.com   www.teachervision.com

Teachers at Random

Let the literary savants at Random help organize your curriculum according to grade level and the calendar year. This site offers a plethora of information about books and authors as well as additional web resources. An obvious, not random choice!

www.TE11.smork.com   www.randomhouse.com/teachers

The U.S. Mint

Help students make heads and tails of coins with this rich resource. Discover lesson plans, unit ideas, and classroom projects on money issues, tailored to History, Language Arts, Mathematics, or Science. Try fun activities like the class penny quilt and spinning nickels. Check out "Teacher Feature" and visit the always-open online library.

www.TE12.smork.com
www.usmint.gov/kids/index.cfm?Filecontents=/kids/teachers/index.cfm

What's the Difference Between Rabbits and Hares?

While they look the same (floppy ears, long incisors, beady eyes), hares are bigger than rabbits. They are also born with a full coat of hair, while rabbits are born hairless and blind.
A young hare is called a leveret, while a young rabbit is called a bunny.
Rabbits live underground in burrows, while hares like to hide among plants. Rabbits prefer to live in groups, while hares are more solitary.

Can they tell each other apart?

Facts courtesy of Ask Earl, website at www.yahooligans.com/content/ask_earl/20010508.html

Ask Earl

Why do dogs spin in circles before they lay down? How do mountains form? What's the difference between a nut and a seed? Earl and Stray Kat have the answers to these questions and hundreds more. Dazzle everyone with little-known facts about just about everything. (-/+)

www.TS1.smork.com
www.yahooligans.com/content/ask_earl/20010508.html

Ask the Answer Worm!

Girls and boys everywhere will love this crawly critter! S.K. Worm, the official annelid (worm) of the USDA's Natural Resources Conservation Service, will help you get smart about soil. Squirm and wiggle your way through questions about how soil is made, does a worm have parents, why plants like soil, and soil conservation. (-/+)

www.TS2.smork.com
www.nrcs.usda.gov/feature/education/squirm/skworm.html

BrainPop.Com

BrainPop movies make science, health, technology and math fun. Try educational animated movies such as "Acne," "Measuring Circles," and "Braces." BrainPOP characters are older, wiser peers who make concepts easy to understand by sharing their own experiences. Don't miss Brain Pop, BrainBuzzzz, and Brain Squeezers. (+)

www.TS3.smork.com www.brainpop.com

How Stuff Works

This site offers an insider's view of how things work. Learn the mysteries behind things natural and man-made. Choose an in-depth explanation from dozens of topics, such as dancing monsters, video games, ATMS, bridges, computers, chocolate, hypnosis, radios, the stock market, DNA, growing hair, 3D glasses, airplanes and much more. (+)

www.TS4.smork.com www.howstuffworks.com

Morse Code

is a series of dots and dashes or long and short sounds used to send messages. Smork has a message for you!

... ..- .-. ..-. / ... -- .- .-. - --..-- /
... - .- -.-- /... .- ..-. . .-.-

—"surf smart, stay safe" in Morse code.

$y = mx + b$

$\pi = 3.1415926$

CO_2

LearningPlanet.Com

Explore a universe of fun learning at this cool site. There's something for everyone, with sections for grades pre–K, 1–3, and 4–6. Learn your ABCs and 123s or study geography, math, and phonics. LearningPlanet has seasonal sections, worksheets, and homework help. Play lemonade tycoon, math mayhem or the memory game. (-/+)

www.TS5.smork.com www.learningplanet.com/index.asp

Letter Lane

Play Pick-A-Letter at this fun site. Click B and meet Ben, who will take you to sites that begin with "B" like Braille, Brazil, and Bullying. Visit Roller coasters, Rainbows and Recycling with Rashad. Let Zach take you to Zoos, Zebras, and Zoboomafu. This grab-bag of letters spells hours of fun! (-/+)

www.TS6.smork.com www.letterlane.com

SYVUM—Online Learning and Interactive Education Activities, Games, and Quizzes

Play games, do activities, take quizzes and learn all kinds of things about almost every subject including math, science, Spanish, French, and even Japanese. Syvum keeps track of your answers, so you can see your score right after you finish. Each activity tells you what age level it's for, so it's easy to pick the right one. (-/+)

www.TS7.smork.com www.syvum.com/squizzes

Sandlot Science

Warning! Hold on to your eyeballs when you click on to this site! Slide and swirl through over 100 illuminating illusions, dimensional distortions and magical mirages. Check out crazy games and card tricks. Build an Illusion Greeting Card and boggle your friends with some brain candy too! (+)

www.TS8.smork.com www.sandlotscience.com

Exploratorium

Calling the curious…take a journey through science. Visit the Hubble Space Telescope, follow a crew of scientists as they hike the slopes of a volcano, discover the science of sports like skateboarding or build your own solar system. Check out the web cams or find a science fair project. (+)
www.VM1.smork.com www.exploratorium.edu

Exploring The Environment—Earth Science Explorer

Exploring the Environment is a cyber museum. Get on the elevator and let the dinosaur take you to the resource room, the earth floor or the dinosaur floor. Each area is filled with all kinds of activities—from cookie recipes to how to make a paper dinosaur to games and lots of useful information for your school projects. (+)
www.VM2.smork.com
www.cotf.edu/ete/modules/msese/elevator.html

Ology

What's Ology? It means the "study of". Learn about ornithology (study of birds), paleontology (study of ancient living things) herpeotology (study of reptiles and amphibians) and just about any OLOGY you can imagine. The coolest scientists around will take you on an amazing tour in any part of this museum. (+)
www.VM3.smork.com www.ology.amnh.org

The Mesoamerican Ballgame

Mesoamerica was home to many advanced civilizations. You'll be astonished when you watch the dangerous ballgame that was played there over one thousand years ago. Explore the nine different cultures of these mysterious people on this award-winning site. Travel back in time to learn about what life was like around the world from 1500 BC to 1590 AD. (+)
www.VM4.smork.com www.ballgame.org

Animal Mates

If you like animals, this is the place for you! Visit this site to download your own desktop pets. They'll perform all kinds of tricks for you at the click of your mouse. Spread some cuddly cheer and send a virtually fuzzy e-card to your friends. (-/+)

www.VP1.smork.com   www.animalmates.com/pets.asp

Neopets

Millions of people have created their own virtual pet here, and now it's your turn. Since you get to choose what your Neopet looks like, and how he or she acts, your virtual pet is all about you. (-/+)

www.VP2.smork.com   www.neopets.com

Virtual Fishtank

SMORK loves this site because you can build-your-own fish, then release it into a huge Virtual FishTank exhibit at the Museum of Science in Boston, Massachusetts. Watch how YOUR fish plays with the other fish in the tank. Go Fish! (-/+)

www.VP3.smork.com   www.virtualfishtank.com/main.html

What Other Kids Have Done

Students from the sixth grade at a private school in New York City gave up a weekend to help raise funds for World Hunger Year. Some of them were on the phone bank during the annual HUNGERTHON radio show.

Fourth Grade students in Kittery, Maine ran a canned food drive at their school and donated the food to the local food pantry. Representatives of the classes helped prepare the food for distribution to the clients of the food pantry.

Facts courtesy of Kids Can Make a Difference, at www.kidscanmakeadifference.org/candu.

The Big Help
This site gives you the chance to help save our water and our planet. Although The Big Help is U.S. based, it has helpful hints for kids across the globe. It provides you with all the info you need for getting started, picking a project and spreading the word. (+)
www.VO1.smork.com
www.nick.com/all_nick/specials/bighelp/how.jhtml?&flashInstalled=true&flashVersion=5

Do Something
Figure out the cause that means the most to you and get involved. Stop discrimination, fight domestic violence, learn suicide and depression facts or speak out about 9-11. These are a few of your options. Do something today! (+)
www.VO2.smork.com   www.dosomething.org

Habitat For Humanity International—Youth Programs
Get rid of homelessness. Help build and fix houses—sort of. Kids under 16 are not allowed to work on construction sites because of US child labor laws. But there are many ways you can help Habitat volunteers like planting gardens and making welcome baskets. Click here to find out more. (+)
www.VO3.smork.com   www.habitat.org/ccyp/youthfact.html

Idealist.org
Idealist.org will guide you to international volunteer sites and show you how to make a difference. The volunteer guide is perfect if you're just starting out. There are also links on how to involve your family and school. Go ahead, point, click, and make the world a better place. (+)
www.VO4.smork.com   www.idealist.org/kat/ktvolunteer.html

IMPORTANT TIP

They want a credit card?

Better check with Mom or Dad or a grown up before doing anything else!

STOP

Kids Can Make A Difference

Kids just like you can help stop world hunger. Learn about what causes hunger and poverty, the people most affected, solutions, and how you can help. Take a hunger quiz and see what other kids are saying. **(+)**

www.VO5.smork.com
www.kidscanmakeadifference.org/candu.htm

National 4-H Council—Are You Into It?

Discover the four H's: head, heart, hands and health. Kids, ages 8 to 18, are invited to learn about volunteering opportunities like helping out at an animal shelter, organizing community clean-ups and recycling programs or fixing up an old building. Find links to local 4-H clubs and other volunteering sites.

www.VO6.smork.com   www.areyouintoit.com

Peace Corps Kids World

What would your day be like if you lived overseas? What kind of food would you eat? Which holidays would you celebrate? What would school be like? What would it be like to be a Peace Corps Volunteer? Explore the world and learn about making a difference. **(-/+)**

www.VO7.smork.com   www.peacecorps.gov/kids

Junior Achievement

All across America, Junior Achievement (JA) pairs kids like you with adults who want to educate and inspire young people. Discover the value free enterprise, business, and economics. Visit this site for information on JA in your area, and learn how your parents, teachers, and other adults can volunteer. **(-/+)**

www.VO8.smork.com   www.ja.org

One of the best things about travelling is all the great food.

If you're in Japan, you can have sushi.

And in the Middle East, hummus bi taheeni, a chick pea based sauce served with crackers, is popular.

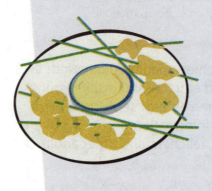

or in Malaysaia, you can try satay, an Asian-style kabob, served with peanut sauce.

Canku Ota (Many Paths)

Celebrate the traditions and cultures of Native Americans, Alaskan Natives, and First Nations people. Did you know that there are over 500 tribes in the United States alone —and many more in Canada? Enjoy the wonderful stories, poems and art. Read about the children and schools on their reservations. (+)

www.WC1.smork.com   www.turtletrack.org

Cities.Com

Learn about the architecture of Addis Ababa, the trade industry in Macon, or the cuisine of Safranbolu with Cities.Com's searchable database of 3791 cities in 149 countries. Find information on music, art, travel tips, maps, local lore and much more. Search by city name or click on the interactive map. (+)

www.WC2.smork.com   www.world-capital.com

CountryReports.org

Get current information on countries all over the world, from Aruba to Laos to Zimbabwe and everywhere in-between. Find info on each country's economy, geography, government, people, and national anthem lyrics. Look at flags, check current weather worldwide, get homework help or log onto an international student exchange. (+)

www.WC3.smork.com   www.countryreports.org

Culture Quest World Tour

Become a virtual globetrotter. Experience the sights, holidays and games of different cultures. Sample traditional country recipes and create unique crafts. Read folktales or discover the many museums and national parks that can be found around our world. (+)

www.WC4.smork.com
http://aristotle.si.umich.edu:2000/div/kidspace/cquest

DID YOU KNOW?

Next time you're having a vanilla ice cream cone, think about this:

About 75 percent of the world's vanilla is grown in Madagascar, the Comoros, and the Réunion—all island nations in the Indian Ocean, off the east coast of Africa. Most of the rest comes from Mexico, Uganda, or French Polynesia.

Courtesy of the World Almanac for Kids at www.worldalmanacforkids.com

Mr. Dowling's Electronic Passport
This site is totally global. With a click of your mouse you can travel to China, the Middle East, Canada, Mexico, and many other places, or explore the historic worlds of Ancient Greece and Colonial Africa. Study guides, homework assignments and exams are free and available for you to print or download. (+)
www.WC5.smork.com   www.mrdowling.com/index.html

The Greatest Places
See and hear the world on this great site. Choose from Songs, Photos, Videos and Sounds. Sing along to a song from another country, hear running water from the Amazon River, or see a lemur leaping in Madagascar. You can even zoom in and out on a scene in QuickTime Virtual Reality.
www.WC6.smork.com
www.greatestplaces.org/medias/media_html/top.html

Kids Web Japan
What would it be like to live in Japan? Explore the details of Japan's climate, daily life, history, culture, inventions, environment, schools, and folk legends. Learn what arigato means, what kids do to preserve traditional Japanese arts like noh and kendo, and how to make Japanese food. (-/+)
www.WC7.smork.com   www.jinjapan.org/kidsweb

The Odyssey
Take an around-the-world Internet field trip. Follow a team of cultural and historical explorers as they travel to Guatemala, Peru, Zimbabwe, Mali, Egypt, Israel, Turkey, Iran, India, and China. You can access the stages of their voyages, and gain a deeper understanding of world cultures. (-/+)
www.WC8.smork.com   www.worldtrek.org/odyssey

Scholastic—Myths From Around The World

Discover different cultures, rich traditions and interesting peoples around the world by exploring their myths—then write your own. Participate in a five-step myth-writing workshop for kids or use the Myth Brain Storming Machine to come up with ideas. Best of all, publish your myths online in Scholastic's Myth Anthology. (+)

www.WC9.smork.com
http://teacher.scholastic.com/writewit/mff/myths.htm

World Almanac for Kids

There's a lot to get smart about here! Join millions of kids from across the world and access fantastic facts about animals, environment, historical birthdays, inventions, nations, presidents, space, and much more. See how history fits together—visit the U.S. History Timeline. There are games, quizzes, and contests too. (-/+)

www.WC10.smork.com www.worldalmanacforkids.com

Turtle Talk—Fun Facts About Hawaii

Aloha! What could be more fun than building a snowman in tropical weather, exploring a volcano or listening to a snail sing? Come and learn about Hawaiian wildlife and culture. Read about Hawaii's history and famous legends. Play games or get some great craft ideas. (+)

www.WC11.smork.com www.tammyyee.com/turtletalk.html

Five Grosser than Gross Animal Facts

1 Many bird parents regurgitate (that means "throw up") into their babies' mouths to feed them.

2 Some animals urinate on their own legs to cool off.

3 Sea cucumbers shove their guts out of their bottoms when scared.

4 Flies taste things, like your sandwich, with their feet. Then they regurgitate. That turns the food to goo, so they can suck it up.

5 Hagfish are tub-like fish that ooze slime. They latch onto the eyeballs, gills or bottoms of other fish and suck their gills out.

Courtesy of Saint Louis Zoo at www.stlzoo.org

Awesome Internet Sites for Kids

Saint Louis Zoo
Let your mouse guide you through this online zoo adventure. Explore the River's Edge Exhibit and get an inside look at the world of animals, or click onto the Trail Map to view the zoo's inhabitants. These remarkable animal pages offer important facts as well as pictures. Go ahead and zoo-m in! (+)
www.ZO1.smork.com www.stlzoo.org/home.asp

San Diego Zoo: Kid Territory
Go wild learning about burrowing owls, baby hippos, or crazy crocodiles. Find out what animals eat and get funny animal facts. Try Dr. Zoolittle's fun experiments like creating giraffe spit. Check out Zoo Job Profiles, play online zoo games, make crafts, or get recipes for monkey muffins and elephant eggs. (-/+)
www.ZO2.smork.com www.sandiegozoo.com/wildideas/kids

Sedgwick County Zoo
Visit this online exhibit of amphibians, birds, fishes, mammals and reptiles. Read about their physical characteristics, diet, behavior, habitat and where they live at the Sedgwick County Zoo. Learn about veterinary medicine, take a Jungle Adventure, or click the Multimedia button to watch a slide show. (-/+)
www.ZO3.smork.com www.scz.org/fun/home.html

ZooWeb
ZooWeb has lots of information on wildlife, aquariums, zoos and more. Check out the ZooCams where you can peek in and see gators, gorillas, pandas and lots of other great zoo animals in action. Visit the Zooper site of the week, and see what's new and cool in zoo sites. (-/+)
www.Z04.smork.com www.zooweb.net

Sandra Antoniani

President, Research, Writing

Sandra practiced criminal law for 10 years before turning to writing and publishing. She left her home in Toronto in 2001 to work with her husband Roger Abbiss on the production of an internet guide in New York City. That venture inspired the creation of SMORK. Sandra now lives on a farm in the Dundas Valley, Ontario, with her husband and their two dogs.

Lisa Slage Robinson

Editor in chief, research, writing

Lisa Slage Robinson is a mother, writer, and lawyer. She earned a B. A., cum laude, in International Studies and Economics from Bowling Green State University and a J. D. from Case Western Reserve University. Ms. Robinson practiced commercial litigation in both the United States and Canada before taking an extended sabbatical to raise her two daughters, ages 6 and 8. She wrote for and edited the *Best of the Best Internet Guide 2002*. Her articles and short stories have appeared in a variety of magazines including *Brides* and *Woman's World*.

Robyn Rektor

Writer, research

Robyn D. Rektor currently works as a writer in Washington, D.C. She holds a B.A. in English and an M.A. in Expository Writing and has taught English and writing at the high school and college levels, edited a newspaper for a non-profit organization, and wrote and edited for a creative services firm. Robyn's preferred use of free time is traveling to explore new places and to discover new finds.

Fiona Rowan

Research, writing

Fiona Rowan is an educator, a researcher and a freelance writer. Her previous publications include Internet guides and academic materials. She has lived in Melbourne, London, New York and Toronto and travels extensively. Ms. Rowan is presently a part time French professor at a community college in Ottawa, Canada. Her next adventure is as of yet undetermined, but she longs to travel again soon and immerse herself in another culture.

Deanna Phillips

Research, writing

Deanna lives in Toronto with her husband and their two daughters. She's an active volunteer in her community and with her childrens' schools. Previously an Activation Coordinator for Senior's, she now enjoys raising her daughters and freelance work from home. A third internet-related book Deanna is involved in will be published in early 2003.

Laurie Smith

Research, Marketing/New Product Development

Laurie Smith has four children. She enjoys being a dedicated member of school and school board committees. Her diverse professional experience includes product design/ development, manufacturing and marketing in Canadian and International markets. Laurie's expertise and passion for horticulture and design are reflected in her home and gardens. She hopes her future holds enjoying times with family and friends and travel adventures to exotic destinations.

Terri Lee

Graphic designer, illustrator

Terri recently graduated as a Graphic designer from George Brown College in Toronto, Canada. Terri's work has been exhibited at the Design Xchange in Toronto, and has also been selected by Applied Arts Magazine for Best Student Work:2001, in a nation-wide competition. Currently, Terri works at a small design house. She also freelances, creating logos, brochures, and illustrations. *Awesome Internet Sites for Kids* is Terri's first entry into book design.

Acknowledgments

A GREAT BIG Thank you to Roger Owen Abbiss without whose advice, encouragement and financial support this project would not have been possible.

Many thanks to Trudy Fraser for her generous input during brainstorming sessions to construct the framework for this project, for her infectious enthusiasm during our continent-wide conference calls, and for her contribution to the writing and research in our Health and Sports categories.

Heartfelt thanks for the wonderful contributions of the Principal and Teaching Faculty at River Heights Public School (Caledonia, ON, Canada), who took the time to consider our project and to send many fabulous sites and ideas, dozens of which have been included in this book.

Thank you to Caroline Robinson, who started us on a vision of SMORK with her artwork, and to Josie Cuzzaniti, who conspired with us for many hours to help find character we were looking for. Both artists' SMORK renditions are included in the body of the book.